RIPE

21ST CENTURY ESSAYS
David Lazar and Patrick Madden, Series Editors

RIPE
ESSAYS

Negesti Kaudo

MAD CREEK BOOKS, AN IMPRINT OF
THE OHIO STATE UNIVERSITY PRESS
COLUMBUS

Copyright © 2022 by The Ohio State University.

All rights reserved.

Mad Creek Books, an imprint of The Ohio State University Press.

Library of Congress Cataloging-in-Publication Data

Names: Kaudo, Negesti, author.

Title: Ripe : essays / Negesti Kaudo.

Other titles: 21st century essays.

Description: Columbus : Mad Creek Books, an imprint of The Ohio State University Press, [2022] | Series: 21st century essays | Summary: "Essays at the intersection of race, sexuality, and pop culture that confront Kaudo's experience as a Black woman and ask what it means to own one's Blackness when contemporary white America simultaneously denigrates and appropriates Black culture"— Provided by publisher.

Identifiers: LCCN 2021038524 | ISBN 9780814258187 (paperback) | ISBN 0814258182 (paperback) | ISBN 9780814281871 (ebook) | ISBN 0814281877 (ebook)

Subjects: LCSH: Kaudo, Negesti. | African American women—Social conditions. | African American women—Social life and customs. | Racism. | African Americans in popular culture. | Whites—Race identity.

Classification: LCC E185.86 .K38 2022 | DDC 305.48/896073—dc23/eng/20211116

LC record available at https://lccn.loc.gov/2021038524

Cover design by Angela Moody

Text design by Juliet Williams

Type set in ITC Century

♾ The paper used in this publication meets the minimum requirements of the American National Standard for Information Sciences—Permanence of Paper for Printed Library Materials. ANSI Z39.48-1992.

*For Nia, and every other Black girl
who learned to bloom in the dark*

CONTENTS

SEED

ACKNOWLEDGMENTS

I've poured my heart and soul into this book, and there are so many people who have helped breathe life into this collection over the several years I've been working on it.

Kristen Elias Rowley, Patrick Madden, and the rest of the editors, publicists, proofreaders, etc. on the team at Mad Creek Books—I'm forever grateful that you chose to house these words amongst your brilliant collection and fell in love with these pieces when they were still being revised. I still can't believe it.

David Lazar—you've believed in me and these essays since day one, and I cannot put into words my gratitude and appreciation for helping me continue to revise, prepare, and submit these pieces for publication. Thank you for furthering my love for the essay, in all its forms.

T. Fleischmann, Jenny Boully, Sasha Hemon, Aviya Kushner, and Sam Weller—so many drafts, so many revisions, so many conversations, and so much reading. I am all the better for it, thank you.

Tim, Sadaf, Gretchen, Amber, Rukmini, Sophie, and Madiha—you all saw most of these pieces when they were sparks and helped me fan the flames with countless discussions over coffees and on trains, with back-and-forth emails for editing, and the most incredible workshop feedback one could ask for. If we had a mascot, I would shout it out here, but just know that you all are the reason I consider Chicago home.

Tori, Courtney, Desiree, Roslyn, Haydée, C. M. Burroughs, and Matthew Shenoda—it is very difficult to write about Blackness when you are the only Black voice in a room. Thank you for your perspectives, conversations, and guidance; these essays benefit from knowing each one of you.

David Weaver and Ohioana Library Association—The Walter Marvin Rumsey Grant was the first award I ever won and one of the most important moments of my writing career. Thank you for choosing me and my work, for believing in my future as a writer, and for embracing me in the Ohio literary community ever since. I am honored to be the youngest recipient and to serve on the board.

Avery, Afa, Hananah, Regan, Laura, and the rest of the staff and residents at The Ragdale Foundation—this book would not be completed without having been afforded the space and time to work amongst you all in the Lake Forest prairie. Session 11 2019 forever.

Emily and Nya—you both became my go-to readers and listeners, and I cannot express the gratitude I have for the both of you as fellow writers, readers, and lovers of workshopping.

Ben, Vanessa, Christine, Mikaylo, Brei, and Mariah—we were trapped at home in the midst of the chaos that was 2020, and you all kept me writing, reading, and thinking. So grateful to know you all and enjoy the glow of your creative energy.

Robert, Leslie, Adam, Josh, and Sonya—you all helped make CCAD feel like home and I could not have completed this collection without the conversations I've had with all of you and my amazing students over the years.

Megan, Jackie, and Jan—I miss the days of Rosé Friday, low-lit editorial meetings, and discussing art, pop culture, and writing every day at work. Thank you for collaborating with me (literally!) as writers, artists, and lovers of art.

Meanwhile (Megan, Jan, and Cat), Chimera (Rozina, Sarah, and Scott), Junior Varsity (Annabel and Alex), Winter Tangerine Workshop (Xandria, Siaara Freeman, and A. Tony), Paging Columbus (Paige, Hannah, and Anisa), The Red Wheelbarrow, *Broad & High*, Columbia College Chicago, and CCAD—I have performed, read, or workshopped several of the pieces included in this collection in spaces you've provided to the audiences and fans you have built by your own creative energy and excitement about art. Thank you for inviting me into your spaces and celebrating my work.

Tita Ramirez, Drew Perry, Cassie Kircher, Kevin Boyle, and Kathy Lyday—can you even believe it? Thank you for introducing me to the essay and providing me space to explore writing, literature, and being creative on the page. Thank you for having contemporary authors on your syllabi instead of the classics. Thank you for making sure poor grammar didn't ruin my work. I would not be the writer and teacher I am today without you all and the rest of the English department at Elon.

Kelly Zavotka, Catherine Dison, Craig Jones, Yolanda Johnson, and Dr. James Allen—without your guidance, interest, and genuine care, I would not have been able to hone my writing and reading skills as a student. I have always loved reading and writing, but you all helped me love teaching and learning, as well.

Jasmine, Michael, and Catie. Catie and Charity. Raven, Vaughn, DaVonti', Chinonso, and Kam. Kelsey, Juan, Christian, Sydney, and Kyle. Mags. Jordan. Jess, Jamiece, Tyrell, Najm, Meghan, and Dirk. And anyone else who heard me say "I'm writing a book," sat and wrote with me, tossed around ideas with me, read drafts, recommended books, or witnessed first-hand the chaos that was my mid-twenties—thank you for help-ing me get through it with laughter, good vibes, and a lot of great company.

My family, literally, all of you—for supporting my work and writing career from my radical angsty teen days to today.

Mom—for instilling in me the love of literature and words at a young age, for passing on the writing gene, and for allow-ing me to put all my eggs in the humanities basket: Writing could have stayed a hobby, but you encouraged me to morph it into a career.

Brea—my hype-woman, my soulmate, my Pisces family by everything but blood. Thank you for all the times you got excited about my work and success when I didn't know how, and thank you for believing in my work. ILY.

Nia—this is for you, my day one (since you showed up). There is nothing stronger than the love I have for you and the admiration I have for the woman you've become. You've sup-ported my work since the awful days of hasty composition notebook poetry, and you were the first person to read this manuscript. Thank you for believing in every word and punc-tuation mark on these pages.

There are too many people I love and respect who weren't on this earth long enough to hold this book in their hands, but especially Ashley Marie Crockett and Edward Joseph Gaines II—I wouldn't be who I am (literally) without both of you. Thank you for all the love you shared with me in the time we had together.

MARGINALIA

Dear reader, this text may be uncomfortable, inaccessible—consider your presence an intrusion.

Stop reading.

Now you know better than to treat people like that. Girl, if you don't open up this page and let them read it. You don't own this space; you are simply renting it. This is not your home. You don't have a home.

Right, my mistake.

JK JK Just kidding. Of course you're welcome here, look at this space, this clearly isn't mine. I know where I'm intended to be: in the one-inch borders of the page, but why would I waste all this white space? The text is black. So, the text must be mine? Let's try something different: Open up for me and I will spoon-feed my words to you, or rather, I can place each letter on your tongue one-by-one and maintain eye contact as you swallow.

I will wait to see if you choke.

•

After black people had everything, and before they had something once again, there were white men transforming into black men for an audience. Minstrels. And minstrels were ignorant, minstrels were superstitious, minstrels were happy, minstrels jigged. Minstrels behaved how slave owners imagined their slaves did once the cotton was picked, and they were sleeping thirty-six bodies to a ten-by-ten space.

I think there is a man in half-black face on a collage at my school outside of the elevators to my workplace. I stare at him with his half-painted, half-bearded face, and I'm sure of it. But the photo is black and white, which gives him the benefit of the doubt—the dark color could be red, blue, green, purple, but my gut tells me it is black.

I bought a drugstore lipstick once and my sister said I looked like a minstrel, so I hastily wiped it off in the car mirror with fast-food napkins.

I said "after black people had everything" to remind you that at first, African people were given away as a form of punishment by more powerful Africans, but never returned. Eventually, they were abducted—chained and stowed on boats as property or objects of trade. And as they lay on each other crossing the Atlantic, they were rocked by waves and covered with shit and piss and vomit and blood. Those who could jump, did, sometimes taking their linked companions with them.

Can an ocean exist as hallowed ground?

Contemporary forms of blackface: makeup, tanning lotion, charcoal masks, body paint, Obama Halloween masks.

Shades of makeup I wear: dark cocoa, medium cocoa, dark deep, 8.5, 65 deep dark ebony. Am I making myself blacker? Is there anything blacker than heritage?

When I was little, I was the only black girl in my class at my private school for four years. My mother tells stories of my white classmates calling me beautiful and wishing they had dark skin like mine.

But I remember being drawn by my best friend as standing alone under the moon on a black-blue background with red lips while she and the rest of our friends basked in the sunlight.

Was I a minstrel or an outcast?

At about eighteen months, children begin to recognize themselves as a self. In the mirror, they will stop touching their reflections and begin to touch their own bodies.

At eighteen months old, I'd been speaking for fifteen months. I already had a sense of self, calling from my crib: "Come get the baby," and cheering myself on. And I exist in Polaroid pictures, in which I faded from white into color, staring into the camera, staring past the camera.

There is a photo of me being held by my father as an infant. I am in a yellow onesie, and he is shirtless with a silver ankh hanging from his neck. My father looks down at me, as I stare past him into the lens. I imagine that I am looking at my mother—my safety, my nurturance.

Black people have been staring into the lenses of cameras since their invention. Slaves in the periphery of family portraits, watching viewers centuries later, unsmiling.

I was surrounded by blackness as a baby. When did I recognize that I was black—or rather, that there was something other than blackness?

When do children recognize race? When do children recognize that there are others? When do children begin to point out that another child is an other?

I was ten when someone pointed out to me that I was other. But it wasn't race. Two white boys told me I was poor, that I was on scholarship, that I didn't belong.

I'm sure I always knew I was black. But maybe the people around me did not think about being white. Maybe they did not know what being white meant.

Can we stop arguing that race is nothing but a social construct? Society has cemented it as a borderline.

In tenth grade, my best friend and I answered a poll in a museum with "I don't see in color, I only see awesomeness," and we dropped our card into a box of folded answers. I felt wrong; just because we were comfortable together didn't mean that I was always comfortable. She was white; I was black. We'd nicknamed ourselves Coffee and Cream.

In 2004, after hearing Kanye West's "All Falls Down," I searched for Emmett Till in the library. I stared at his face, no longer a face. I remember realizing I'd never get the image out of my head.

I understood what death meant. I did not yet know hate.

In second grade, a Jewish girl's parents told her I was ghetto. Later, in fifth grade, another black girl and I read a page in our social studies textbook over and over because it said that during the Holocaust, Jewish people were forced into ghettos. We said, *They can't possibly mean our ghetto.* They didn't.

Ghetto—originally used in Venice to describe segregated Jewish communities, of course, there were the Nazi ghettos, and then there were the ones in the United States for European immigrants (think Chicago's Pilsen, Little Italy, Ukrainian Village), but now ghetto is synonymous with poor, with black.

Trace it back to prejudice and racism.

My "ghetto" neighborhood, Linden, Columbus, Ohio, is just a middle-class suburban area inhabited by lower-middle- and middle-class black families.

One thing I did not learn about in my home: the Ku Klux Klan. When is it appropriate to tell a little black girl that adult white men and women hate her? I only found out in seventh grade because someone tagged the exterior brick of our school with KKK and other racist things. A Jewish girl was fidgeting and staring at me all morning. I knew I should've been afraid, but instead I was fascinated.

I guess death has always been right there as a possibility. Stalking me in my own shadow.

RIND

ETHER

THE ANGRY BLACK WOMAN is an American myth come to life. She is a chimera of black women depicted in media created for and saturated with white people. She exists as a possibility—or rather, an expectation—of non-black people to resurrect itself at any given moment. Because of her, I must police myself in public. I don't have cultural permission to express anger or fear. Society has repossessed my emotions, as if I owe them even more of my humanity, cashing in an IOU for what? Freedom?

In the 1930s, a radio show called *Amos 'n' Andy* created the foundation for the public mythos of the angry black woman. At its inception, Amos and Andy were two black men voiced by two white men; in its truest form, *Amos 'n' Andy* was an audio minstrel show. But in 1939, adding to plot, the two men introduced the character Sapphire Stevens: a black woman who constantly nagged, manipulated, and emasculated her husband, Kingfish. Sapphire was voiced, and later portrayed on *The Amos 'n' Andy Show*, by Ernestine Wade, a black actress from Jackson, Mississippi, who grew up in LA. For Wade, Sapphire was the role of a lifetime, and she was proud to portray her. Culturally, Sapphire became a negative stereotype, and versions of her continue to appear in television, movies, and music to this day. It's because of Sapphire and her legacy that many black women end up labeled as loud, rude, opinionated, and negative by our peers. People learn from what we interact with and consume, and for centuries, black women have been mythologized in the United States by white men and women as both a threat and inferior—a contradiction. The gap between the stereotypes "Mammy" and "Sapphire" is large enough to ask the question: How did black women morph from the preferred and most suitable primary caretakers of white children to volatile and threatening women ready to conquer white men at any moment? Could it be a repercussion of being freed from slavery? Or is it deeper: a tactic of using Sapphire as a way to attack black men by implying that they can't control their women, that they are weak when their women are strong, that while a black woman has no place, neither does the black man?

I used to be angry. I was consumed by so much anger that I couldn't release in my everyday environments: My private, predominantly white institutions couldn't handle it; my mother wouldn't allow it; and when you scream in an open field for no reason, there's always a risk someone will call the cops. Instead, I listened to a lot of Eminem. My mother played *The Eminem Show* in the car, so I grew up singing along to Eminem's emotional crises. Eminem was angrier than me, and as a white man, it was socially acceptable for him to publicly vent that anger. I sat in corners with my headphones blasting songs about him hypothetically murdering his ex-wife, hating his mother, and being plagued by demons. I've never been ashamed to admit that I found something soothing in his anger—I envied it.

There are privileges that come with whiteness, and one of those is emotional range without consequence. And maybe that's why in film and television, it's never shocking when a white male protagonist slams his fist through the drywall in a fit of anger, or when a white woman claws at another's hair or tosses a drink across the table. It's never "anger," instead, these moments are described with different words. *Real Housewives* is full of "drama." *Real World* gets "real." White supremacy is now a form of counterprotest and scandal, not hate—at least, in the United States. And of course, there was Forty-Five sitting at his large empty desk with access to the nuclear codes, using Twitter to rant and rave instead of running the country. He is the pinnacle of what happens when white privilege, ignorance, and anger combine. The privilege of white anger—white rage—is being able to walk away from confrontations unscathed, being able to breathe easily, being able to shed emotional outbursts like skin cells.

To me, the angry black woman stereotype is all based in rhetoric. The "angry" defines the "black woman" through active-voice phrasing. Whereas in passive voice, "angry" becomes reasonable, temporary in a sentence such as "the black woman is angry." And rhetoric can be tricky; English grammar is difficult, but I've never heard anyone use the phrase "angry white woman." Tomi Lahren, Ann Coulter, and Laura Ingraham are not angry women. They are *passionate* about conservative Republican politics; they are patriots. They are not aggressive or intimidating, words my peers have used to describe me, which I assume is because positive words, like "ambitious" and "determined" are translated through a racialized, grammatical lens in which a black woman doing well for herself (and thus, better than others) is a threat. When I display genuine emotion, I am flattened into a concept: angry black woman, poor black woman, ghetto, ratchet, bougie, mean, rude. When a white woman feels something, she becomes more dynamic, four-dimensional.

Last week, an angry white woman flipped off my Lyft driver for blocking the entrance to Trader Joe's. You're probably thinking, *Angry, why would you describe her as angry? She was probably frustrated, annoyed—maybe she wanted to get to her hummus faster.* No. Last week, an angry white woman, who was not in the turning lane for Trader Joe's, flipped off my Lyft driver and me and my friend, while we were getting into the car at the entrance of Trader Joe's. We are all people of color. And my Lyft driver, instead of reciprocating her anger, attempted to talk to said white woman, but she continued to aggressively point and shout at us from the safety of her black SUV before speeding off when the light turned green. That's anger, right?

But, I guess we're lucky.

Sometimes, that story ends your life.

It's a fact that everyone gets angry, though anger exists in different forms. I have made many a white person angry, and usually it happens when I say the word "no." And that's where privilege of anger appears. No: two letters, one sound; a soft consonant nuzzling a short vowel. Because marginalized people weren't ever intended to have the privilege of saying no. No, you can't say the n-word. No, you can't be mad that Black Panther is a black superhero. No, you can't attend a women's-only screening of *Wonder Woman*. No, you cannot have sex with me. No, that's racist. No, that's sexist. No, I don't want or need your help.

Once, I said "no" to a white man and it ended our entire friendship. He was shocked. I was not. After the third time of me repeating "no," he stared at me in disbelief, and said, "After everything I've done for you?"

As if he were my husband, my father, my master. As if I would answer his next request by falling to my knees and pleading, "yes!" As if I were docile, submissive.

Anger can be simple. Anger can run deep. It can curdle in your veins.

Maybe I wasn't even angry, maybe my sadness just manifests that way. I was sad for a lot of reasons: My dad was dead, my family was poor, my cousins were moving away, boys didn't like me, I was bullied, I was ugly, on and on and on. But my sadness was invalidated by my privileged peers, whose access to therapists and psychiatrists allowed them to brag about diagnoses of clinical depression and anxiety, to brag about their problems, which I don't mean to invalidate, but none of them were also burdened with the stress of being poor and black. How many of them had their access to water turned off and were forced to handwash their clothes in an old pot of boiled water? Which of them spent their summers in summer school for a guaranteed meal and childcare? How many of them had to fall asleep to candlelight, praying the house wouldn't catch on fire because the power had been cut off? How many of them watched the repo man take away the family car?

Do they know how stressful that is? I am constantly having to consider every facet of my identity before making a decision. Fear of the consequences of a single misstep, mistake, misunderstanding always present in the back of my mind.

But to them, I was "dramatic."

This one time in college, I yelled at a white girl because she told a boy not to knock on my door. And it wasn't just her, but a whole day of things bothering me, pushing me closer and closer to an edge I'd danced on before. It just happened to be this girl who pushed me off it—wait, I shouldn't say pushed.

For me, anger builds up over days, weeks, sometimes months. And I'm comfortable dancing on the edge of rage because it takes a lot for me to go there. But when I do, it can be draconian, spilling out in a verbal assault: a list of issues, moments, and flaws all directed at the misfortunate person that took me there.

My sister says my underlying anger is like ether. Like Nas's four-minute-thirty-seven-second diss track—born out of necessity—to put Jay-Z back in his place. Nas's "Ether" exists like the final combo in a game of *Mortal Kombat*, right when the narrator screams, "Finish him!" It's out of character, it is a glimpse—ether to burn, ether as a metaphorical straitjacket for a competitor. Later, Nas said in an interview, "I was told a long time ago, ghosts and spirits don't like the fumes from ether, and I just wanted to affect [Jay-Z] with my weapon and get to his soul."

Nas's weapon is rap. Mine is language.

Ether, like the flammable organic compound that turns solids into liquids. Ether, the anesthetic.

I'll dance on the edge of rage and swan dive into it, just to let you know I'm not the one to provoke.

So anyways, this girl in college had my name in her mouth, so I swung my door open and everyone in the hallway scattered except for her doing dishes in our kitchenette. And I asked her why she would tell someone not to talk to me if they were looking for me, and she said, "Because I knew you were mad." And I hadn't been mad; I was frustrated, irritated, annoyed. But when you *assume* I'm mad, that makes me mad. She'd assumed. She'd wanted to quarantine me, isolate me— angry black woman as pariah. And we stared at each other: me in my doorway and she in the kitchenette, and I started telling her off.

Common sense things, like: You don't tell anyone what the fuck to do. You don't tell people not to talk to me. You have no right to make decisions for me. You keep my name out of your fucking mouth.

And while drying a dish, she lets me know that she doesn't like the language that I'm using. My leap into rage is graceful, it is an Olympic dive, it is a single drop of ether falling to catalyze an explosion. I blacked out. And gripping the countertop, I screamed at her, my body trembling, as I repeated, "Say something!" Just begging her to say the wrong thing. But she only stared at me. A smile twitched at the corner of her lips. Infuriated, I called her a cunt; played into her insecurities by reminding her that no one liked her, and she had no friends. I went back into my room and found my door handle had put a hole in the wall from the force of me swinging it open.

This was not the first time I experienced a rage blackout (scientifically viewed as a form of dissociation) while yelling at a white woman, and it wouldn't be the last. It happened a few times in high school and middle school, when my anger was managed by isolation and Eminem. Because, for some unknown reason, people (boys and girls, black and non-black) loved to publicly tell me off, maybe thinking I was too weak to defend myself. Their mistake.

A blackout rage is like an orgasm of anger—the buildup sucks, but the release is great. In the same way tears are cathartic, I imagine that me blacking out while telling someone off provides the same purging of emotions. Except afterwards, I only vaguely remember what I said. And people are always staring at me like I've done something wrong, while I feel better than ever.

The people who witnessed my blackout rage in college said they thought I was going to rip the kitchenette counter from the linoleum. After that, they labeled me "the crazy bitch," "the one not to fuck with," or "the one to have on your side." And while most of that was true, I did not want to be known as the crazy bitch.

Crazy, which is just another word for mad, which is just another word for angry. Bitch, somehow black women always end up as "bitches," especially if we show any emotion. I'm not an angry black woman. There is no such thing as an angry black woman—she is a fable. I'm not on my period. I don't hate *everything* and I'm not hungry. I'm frustrated and tired. But if I dare express my feelings, I am "too emotional," "dramatic," "sensitive," or "crazy." So, I bottle up my emotions, leading to more frustration, irritation, and eventually anger. Sometimes I'm angry, sometimes I'm sad, but mostly I wish my emotions could be disconnected from the fact that I am black and a woman.

What is privilege, if not complaining when black women display real emotion? Of course we're angry, there's a lot of shit we don't and can't have or are condemned if we do. Why should I be expected to explain my emotions when they boil over, when white men and women can explode without consequence? There are hundreds of videos of white women cussing out mall employees because their card was declined, they were caught shoplifting, or the cashier is a person of color; white teachers threatening students when they're frustrated in the classroom; or white men ripping doors off the hinges during fraternity rush week. In extreme cases, white rage can manifest in forms of domestic terrorism and mass murder, white supremacy and genocide; sure, their motives are questioned, but black victims are criminalized or ignored.

We still don't know why a white man shot more than 500 people in Las Vegas in August 2017, an act of terrorism allowed to fall under the radar. We still lack answers to why five women were targeted and executed in a bank in January 2019. A white man is sentenced to death and the judge scoffs at what "a waste" of potential. A white man massacres a Bible study and gets burgers with the cops on the way to jail. A white man massacres a movie theater and he's labeled "troubled." White men storm the Capitol building, and what? We wait until it happens again? If there's anything that history has taught me, it's that white men can get away with anything. But the media refers to murdered black boys as "no angel." They dig up mugshots and criminal records of black victims to validate their deaths, but when Brock Turner raped a woman behind a dumpster, I had to hear and read about his swimming record, his Olympic potential, his Stanford paraphernalia. He only got six months. He was out in three. In my world there is no such thing as justice.

When I screamed at that girl in college, I knew I had fucked up. I had done the one thing black people—black women—aren't supposed to do. I'd gone off on a white girl; I'd manifested the angry black woman. The angry black woman who is apparently angry because she's black and not for any legitimate reason. What has always bothered me about that moment was that girl's calm demeanor, the way she stared at me with her icy blue eyes, seemingly amused at my outburst. And I can recognize that now as security. A security in her status and position as a white woman being screamed at by a black woman; that if anything were to go wrong, she'd be safe, unlike me.

Part of my anger is the composite of generational frustration and bitterness. Black children aren't born angry or broken, but all it takes are small moments of being made aware that you're different—not because you're unique, but because of your class or skin color. I was a happy black child. It wasn't until white children and their parents began pointing out my poverty and skin color that I became frustrated and embarrassed of my life. I was powerless. So, I put my head down and did my work, a lot of reading and listening to try to understand the world around me better. Frustration turns to anger. If left to build, powerlessness and anger evolve into rage.

I've never apologized for being angry and don't plan to. When I'm unspooling, I've learned to confront people with a mild dose of anger: calm tone, brutal honesty, and a smile. Whatever it takes to not black out when someone drives me to that point. I'm a human, not something to just be walked over and disrespected whenever someone feels like it.

Though rage bubbles under the surface like the super geyser in Yellowstone, I haven't had an ether moment in almost a year. Sometimes people push my buttons: assuming my emotions, speaking to me with condescension, lying to me—

all these things that drive me crazy. And I can feel the anger boiling, the blood rushing through my veins. I know the right thing to do is to walk away from these people, teeth clenched, mouth shut, and keep everything I want to say inside. Sometimes, I miss the thrill, the spitefulness, the burn of hurting someone's feelings by doing exactly what they tried to do to me: telling them about themselves. It is a special form of darkness that resides deep inside of me, one that wants to ruin people. Some people deserve to feel the ether. But I swallow it and walk away.

There is something happening with black women, black men, blackness in general. Part of it is increased self-care, part of it is awareness. There's been a change in the atmosphere, where after 400 years, we seem to be on the horizon of getting our due. Of course, every day is a constant battle against inequality, police violence, infidelity, white supremacy, and attacks against one's happiness. But black people have been evolving in the United States ever since we were brought here unwillingly. I think about the ways black women have approached protests: with serenity, peacefulness, a calm but strong presence. The woman in Baton Rouge in the sundress with her arms out to the police in riot gear. Angela Peoples at the Women's March with the sucker in her mouth holding a sign that says: "DON'T FORGET: WHITE WOMEN VOTED FOR TRUMP." My sister, twenty-two years old, standing alone outside of her university president's office, holding a sign above her head for hours.

I wonder how I fit into this equation, how do my words function as a form of resistance, as a reclamation of my blackness, stripping it of stereotypes and negative energy? Possibly into the category of emerging creative black women using their art to illuminate their voices and perspectives. The black women who have taken matters into their own hands, molding emotion into substance, speaking out against injustices and untruths, carving out space in places where we had none. We are digging to the roots of a silenced history: a womanist and activist culture—a promise to reclaim the dignity of our mothers.

HOW TO STEAL
A CULTURE

FIRST, YOU MUST FIND SOMEONE FROM THAT CULTURE who doesn't seem to fit in. Someone who is isolated from her own culture and surrounded by yours. Welcome her with open arms into your life: Invite her into your home, feed her, buy her gifts—spoil her in ways you imagine she's only dreamed about.

Begin with compliments—make sure you exoticize her to the fullest. Tell her you love her skin tone. Make sure to touch her dark skin as much as possible without ever acknowledging the contrast between your fingers and her body. Point out its flawlessness by complimenting her clear skin and asking for her skin regimen. Always bring up how jealous you are that she can sit in the sun without burning. In the summer, be sure to put your arm next to hers and complain about your tan not being close to her complexion. Two weeks later, put your arm next to hers again and nudge her about how soon you'll be darker than her. Don't forget to wink. When she goes inside to nap after lying in the sun for fifteen minutes, hide your envy in jest. Say something like, "We are unworthy, sun goddess" or "Just trying to be like you" as she walks away.

Always make sure to remind her of her body. Chances are, you're smaller than her in the hips or breasts, so offering to share clothes can be both a compliment and an insult—a way to spin your superiority as inferiority. At pre-games and sleepovers, stand in the mirror and critique your body, point out your imperfections and bring up both your bodies as if you could modern-day Frankenstein the two of you together. Something like, "If I had your eyes, boobs, and hips, with my nose and ass . . ." Pause for effect, clarify: "Not that your ass isn't great, it's just so much." And then continue explaining how much of a bad bitch you'd be with her ancestry implanted under your skin.

Once she is your friend, help her assimilate into your culture by explaining that it's correct. Your culture is the one she should admire and want to be a part of. Clarify that it's not white culture, but *American* culture. Introduce her to a new version of her country. Make her want the things you have. Take her shopping at Abercrombie and Fitch, Aéropostale, American Eagle, Banana Republic, J. Crew, and Victoria's Secret. Places where her body won't fit into the clothes without drastic changes. Where petite women in all black, tape measures hanging around their necks, ask if she'd like to be measured. Where employees don't look in her direction. Where noses are up in the air as if something smells bad.

Smother her independence with courteousness. Always take the check at dinner. Pay for the movies. Buy breakfast. Never ask for gas money. Always extend an invitation. Never take no for an answer. Even when she can't afford it, scoff and buy the ticket without her permission. Let her taste the flavors of privilege; mask the sour with *parfum blanc*. And when she leans in close, remind her how sweet it tastes.

In return, ask her about her culture. Where are you from? *Ohio.* No, really, where are you from? *Ohio.* What does your name mean? *Queen.* That's beautiful, where's it from? *It's Ethiopian.* So, you're Ethiopian. *No.* Then, where—and as she explains her background and her family, nod your head as if you're listening. And then go home and google Ethiopia, find it on a map, and see images of dark women with gauges, scars, and babies clinging to their backs. Tell yourself this is her culture, even though it's not.

Gentrify her name. Make it foreign to her tongue. NUH-GUESS-STAY. NUH-GUESS-STEE. NI-JEST-TEE. NUH-JEST-AY. NEE-GEE-STEE. NUH-GEE-STEE. Don't stop until she pronounces it wrong. And then give her a nickname. GUEST. GIST. GUEST-ER. GUESS-TEE. NEHJ-EE. GIGI. Ignore her when she corrects you.

Don't go to her house. Don't visit her neighborhood. You can't be around too many black people at once—you should hit just the right note of not racist, slightly ignorant. Plus, your parents said it's unsafe. Always ask why she's not allowed to have friends over, as if you want to go, but then never ask to visit. Muffle your surprise when she displays any sign of wealth. Struggle to comprehend how regardless of location and class, she has something that you don't. Devalue her property by deeming it as uncool. She bought her phone six months after it was released, it is no longer the one to have. Get everyone on your side. Tell her it's okay. Make sure to have a slight tone of pity offset with a smile. Give her your hand-me-downs without asking if she wants them. Even if she's not, act as if she's poor.

But nothing is free. Culture is not free. White privilege isn't free.

Hide your guilt in public. Always hide the fact that you have nothing to claim besides a history of colonization and conquering. Ignore that you have no culture. Ignore the fact that everything you have is stolen. Turn that guilt and shame into rage. Mold that rage into ignorance. Use it to fuel your racism.

Cut off her dreadlocks in class. Add it to your trophy collection. Pull on her hair when you sit behind her and ask if she can feel it. Ask her how she washes her hair. Tell her that she's dirty. Slide your dirty hands into her hair to feel her scalp without permission. Cover her with insults like sweat: tentacles, spiders, Predator. Years later, try to dread your own hair: throw away your combs. Have a fit when your mother freaks out.

When you are older, you'll realize there are ways to become black while remaining white. Fillers and injections all over your body to sculpt and fill out the areas of your choice. For a price. Turn your body into a hot bag of plastic. Liposuct your insecurities. Learn to twerk because the black girls do it and Miley Cyrus does it. Twerking is the way in, you're sure of it. Kiss a black man and suck his bottom lip. Tell him you love the thickness. Pay someone to use a bee to sting your bottom lip. They sell lip gloss with trace amounts of venom now—use that too.

Listen to the radio religiously. Adopt a language that isn't yours. Affect an accent. Insist that imitation is a form of flattery and that this is imitation, not mockery. Download her culture onto your phone and music player. Sing in your bedroom about drugs, trap houses, hair, poverty, hope, relationships, blackness, blackness, blackness. Listen to those songs over and over, searching for meaning in the lyrics, in the beat, until you know all the words and loudly proclaim: "Thank you, Beyoncé, for gifting this to me." It is the "me" that ricochets off her culture into yours as you have made oppression relatable, oppression fashionable, oppression profitable. Stop censoring yourself at home. Say it: *nigga.* Sing along to "F. U. B. U." by Solange: *All my niggas in the whole wide world / made this song to make it all y'all's turn / for us, this shit is for us.*

Pin your hair back like Solange. Let a bandanna hang from your back pocket. Pay a dentist to install a single diamond in your canine. Flash it in your pictures. Inflate your ass with fat or silicone and then do a handstand with your feet on the wall. Twerk your heart out. See a black man and think, "He's cute for a black guy." Seduce him and place his hand on your ass, hold him by the wrist, and say, "Now, I'm just like a black girl," or "Don't you like that, King?" Or "I've got everything you need." Buy him a pair of shoes. Get on your knees and let him use you. Colonize him while you're on top. When he becomes too much, when he stops obeying, when he no longer works to please you: assert your birthright. And when he doesn't care, say it: *nigger.* Tell him that you'll make him pay. Scream it: *rape.* Move on to another black man. And another. Another. Proclaim yourself Snow Bunny. Salivate at the thought of mixed babies.

Have the audacity to tell your friend that you are blacker than her. Look her in the eyes as you do it. Tell her that you have the best of all worlds: money, power, privilege.

At the end, when you have completed your theft and manipulated her culture into something you can exploit and profit from; when you have built up your privilege using her— when you have lost her, you will chalk it up as a phase. You will revert to white men and claim you've never known love

before. Say, "I'm done with black guys, they're too cocky."
Make excuses. Let your ass shots wear off. Stop plumping
your lips. Return to country music. Wear more white clothing.
Trade in your Jordans or Louboutins for a pair of riding boots.
Never speak to her again. Everything will become black and
white. And you'll be so busy trying to distance yourself, you'll
ignore your own shadow.

KINGS, QUEENS, AND WARRIORS

PEOPLE USED TO TOUCH MY HAIR and ask me if I washed it. I told them I treated my hair the same way they did theirs, except I didn't wash it as often and without a fine-tooth comb. Boys in school would cut my hair without asking to see if I could feel it, knowing that I couldn't because I had dreadlocks. At work, they don't sell any makeup products dark enough for me to wear, but my coworkers always suggested that I use the ones with skin-lightening chemicals in them. When the spray-tan woman visited the office, my coworkers held their rusted arms out against mine in comparison, pouting because I was still darker. They wanted my skin tone because it was pretty, and I smiled, even though we all knew it would never happen. Men tend to hyper-sexualize me because one stereotype of my skin is that I will give it up for anyone. People who are not dark, not a shade of chocolate to coal, consider us a mystery, exotic—are these compliments? I am something—not someone—to touch without permission. Outside of the club one night, a man reached forwards and twirled a single curl on my head with his finger, snatching his hand away before I turned around. I stared at him as I told my friends that people need to keep their fucking cum-covered fingers out of my hair. A man I'd just met in the airport won't stop telling me that I'm beautiful, but three days later, a man walks up and down the street screaming about how ugly I am.

•

I turned on the documentary *Dark Girls* for the first time and lay back on the couch, ready to hear the "real truth" about girls like me and their struggles. *Dark Girls* is about the discrimination that dark-skinned women encounter all over the world, exploring the roots of the discrimination and how it affects women's self-esteem. A little black girl appears on-screen and she doesn't look at the camera, instead playing with her fingers in her lap as the camera zooms in on her face. Someone asks her why she doesn't want to be called black. *Because I'm not black*, she says, and the light behind the camera reflects in her eyes. My white roommate hears this and neglects doing her homework to sit rigidly on the couch opposite of me, gluing her eyes to the screen to hear more about the plight of black women. I don't say anything and continue to watch. I try not to look at her throughout the film, afraid I'll hate her for something she wasn't involved in.

I wonder when one becomes truly aware of one's skin tone for the first time. Is it when you're a little kid and your friends are drawing you under the night sky, instead of gallivanting under the sun with them? Is it when the only color crayon or marker you can use to draw yourself is brown, until Crayola starts getting fancy and comes out with different shades of brown and tan, so you can show whether you're dark-skinned or light-skinned? Is it when you find out someone finds you unattractive because of your skin? Is it when someone loves you because of your skin?

•

I never thought about what it meant to be black. Blackness was secondary to who I was, a skin tone, that's it. It didn't change who I made friends with or who I liked, but that was just me. For others, it was a reason not to like me, not to trust me, to find me unattractive—I was at the bottom of the hierarchy of color totem pole. I don't know why I've started to care and consider it more. Maybe because I've returned to my neo-soul/R&B roots, listening to Lauryn Hill, Erykah Badu, and India.Arie more. Maybe it's because I haven't encountered much writing on being black in my classes, but when I write a character in a fiction story, everyone assumes that they are also black. It might be because I'm falling in love with myself again, after hating myself for so long. It could simply be the fact that Pantene has stopped selling co-wash in stores and my hair is being terribly neglected. Or maybe it's so many black people are being killed lately, and I want to get this off my chest before someone decides I looked at them the wrong way.

Some people hate blackness. They want to watch it burn away from our bodies and bare our milk-white bones as we hang from a cross. They've separated us into shades: dark-skinned and light-skinned. They have found a way to turn black into crime and shame and have linked us back together with metaphorical chains. People keep trying to beat black beneath the dirt before we can grow. Black is the new ugly.

Other people can only see in black and white. They look at me, they wonder how I'm doing it. Others wonder if I'll actually make it, after all, I'm black, and I majored in English and psychology—where could I possibly be going? I've got this afro with red-violet highlights. I have a frown etched into my face. And on top of it all, I'm slathered in this rich, coffee-colored skin that people either hate or love. I'd tell you to ignore it, to not give a fuck about the color of my skin unless you're casting me as character in a show. I try not to care about it, but it's unavoidable, black people and white people alike forcing me think about it.

When I was younger, I lived two different lives. I had to impress two different types of people: I had to prove that I was black, and I had to prove that even so, I was smart, ambitious, and worth something. All the time, people would tell me I wasn't black. White boys who wanted to be cool told me they were *blacker* than me, people told me I didn't *sound* black, white girls told me I didn't *act* black, even my mom told me I was white, once.

"You're so white," she sneered, and I asked her what she meant, but she couldn't articulate it, so I cussed at her, so she hit me. For a moment, I couldn't see anything else but my hands around her throat to defend myself.

Years of rage swelled inside of me before spilling out in a scream: "What does that mean? What does that even mean?"

I didn't know that my skin tone and culture weren't legitimate. I didn't know I was expected not to do well in school, and I didn't know I wasn't supposed to know how to communicate. No one told me that these stereotypes were the rules: This is what makes me black, and this is what makes me white. I didn't know I could even be considered white. Looking at my reflection, I don't see white, tan, or cream. I have only the white of my teeth and the whites of my eyes. If people had their way, I wouldn't be here right now. I wouldn't be spinning this web of stories together, so that everyone can understand what it's like to be excluded from your birthright and not included in the group you've been lumped into. I could end up like this essay: looked over, scribbled on, and molded into what others want with a tiny dash of what the writer intended.

My first name means "Queen of Queens" in Ethiopian. My middle names represent goddesses of the moon and dawn, respectively. My last name is Kenyan, and I'm not sure what it means, the internet fails me here, and it belongs to neither of my parents. I'm black. That's undisputable. A concrete description of myself: My skin tone is a nice, coffee-chocolate color, my nose is stereotypically and ethnically wide; my eyes are the color of soil if you dig deep enough, and I have Louisiana lips (as my mom once said). I spent thirteen years of my childhood and adolescence with dreadlocks because my parents were Rastafarian. Now, I sport a kinky afro in various styles. People take this as a statement, but if they knew any better, they would know it's a veiled laziness because curls are too high maintenance. Very rarely will I conform to society's pressure of having straightened hair to achieve the "clean-cut" look. I wear plus-size clothes, weigh more than I should, and hate my body because I'll never look like dolls I played with growing up, the singers I croon along to, or the women in the magazines.

I'm black. I do not prefer the term African-American unless I am bubbling it in on a form. I don't want to be referred to or categorized as a person of color for your political correctness. I am not some cut-out doll that was simply colored within the lines. My ancestors were once kings, queens, and warriors, but people seem to have forgotten that. Their titles may have been forgotten, but that power is still coursing through my veins and pushing me forward. And if you can't understand that, then there is nothing left for me to say.

~~UN~~BOTHERED

A MICROAGGRESSION

AND WHEN IT HAPPENS, it won't sit with you right. You'll feel a pang in your chest, and you won't be sure if it's anger or sadness. You'll have three options: fight, flight, or—

I bring up the mathematical theory of chaos in my nonfiction class to discuss a book. I am the only black body in this space. Everyone looks at me as if chaos theory does not exist, as if I have made it up on the spot because they don't know it. And for a moment, I think: Maybe I did make it up, maybe I am not as smart as I believe I am, maybe chaos theory doesn't exist—

Next to me, a white man in the room says—not to me, but in the direction of the center of the room—"That must be that Columbus Public School education, right there."

And when it happens, it won't sit with you right. You'll feel a pang in your chest, and you won't be sure if it's anger or sadness. You'll have three options: fight, flight, or—

I am setting up a presentation in class, when a white man says something in passing about being a white man. And I tell him, I wouldn't know because I am not a white man. He looks me in the eyes—piercing blue, Eurocentric beauty—and asks me: "But don't you want to be a white man? You can get everything you want without even trying."

And when it happens, it won't sit with you right. You'll feel a pang in your chest, and you won't be sure if it's anger or sadness. You'll have three options: fight, flight, or—

I am in Albuquerque, New Mexico, for a writing conference. I am here, specifically, to read an essay on race. With me are two other (white) women and our chaperone, a white man (not particularly interested in the conference, but more being in New Mexico). We have taken a taxi to a part of Albuquerque that boasts *Breaking Bad* and Old Town simultaneously. The restaurant is an authentic Mexican restaurant, as authentic as one can get in New Mexico, and we walk in a group of five, asking for a table of five. The manager, from behind the counter sees us and laughs.

"Table for four?" he asks.

"No, five," I say, not paying much attention.

"No, no, table for four. I need a dishwasher." He laughs and points in my direction.

And when it happens, it won't sit with you right. You'll feel a pang in your chest, and you won't be sure if it's anger or sadness. You'll have three options: fight, flight, or—

I have saved up the $300 for the Dr. Dre headphones I want. In the Apple Store in Columbus, Ohio, with my best friend and sister, we are hanging out by the headphones laughing while I survey each pair, making sure that these are the ones I want. A man—an Apple "genius"—walks up to our group and we stop laughing. He looks at me.

"I'm going to need to see your bag." My messenger bag is hanging at my hip, latched closed.

"Why?"

"Someone said that they saw you put a pair of headphones in your bag." My best friend throws her hands up and storms out of the store. My sister follows. I look back down at my bag, still closed and never opened while I was inside the store.

"Who?" I know I don't have to show him the inside of the bag. I know that this mixture of fear and rage is causing my hands to shake and my heart to pound. He points behind me at the "genius" bar: They are all staring at our interaction. A blonde woman turns away. "Why would I steal a pair of headphones when I came here to buy them?"

"I need to see inside your bag—"

And when it happens, it won't sit with you right. You'll feel a pang in your chest, and you won't be sure if it's anger or sadness. You'll have three options: fight, flight, or—

I am in the graduate lounge at school, explaining to my friend that people of color are known to have tighter skin elasticity. I am relating this back to working at a plastic surgery center and reasons why women have labiaplasties. The white woman next to me leans across me to give her input on the subject:

"It's because they wear all that cocoa butter," she laughs.

And when it happens, it won't sit with you right. You'll feel a pang in your chest, and you won't be sure if it's anger or sadness. You'll have three options: fight, flight, or—

A white woman puts her hands on my face. One palm on each cheek. She is drunk; I am not that drunk. My eyes widen. She says: "I just want to *be* you."

And when it happens, it won't sit with you right. You'll feel a pang in your chest, and you won't be sure if it's anger or sadness. You'll have three options: fight, flight, or—

I go to the health center for an ear infection and my doctor is an old white man from Georgia. He asks me about my background, and I tell him I'm from Ohio and he nods, before asking me about my ethnic background. I don't really know my ethnic background, so I tell him I'm a little Creole since my dad was born in Louisiana. The doctor checks one ear for the infection I've already let him know I have.

"Where I'm from, we'd call you a 'redbone.'"

And when it happens, it won't sit with you right. You'll feel a pang in your chest, and you won't be sure if it's anger or sadness. You'll have three options: fight, flight, or—

—sometimes you end up shrinking, deep inside yourself, and you end up lost. Who are you? Why are you here? Why don't they believe you?

And maybe you're wrong, maybe they're right. They become voices in your head. Constantly criticizing you. Mocking you.

You don't deserve to be here. You don't know anything. You're worthless. Everything about you screams inferiority, from the melanin in the cells of your skin to the kinks of your hair. There is a standard of beauty and intellect that you will never meet because of your breeding.

Your options are limited. Are you going to fight them all, a thousand to one, teeth bared and fists at the ready? Beast. Are you going to get in their face and scream, spit flying onto their cheeks with every consonant? Savage. Are you going to remain silent, bite your tongue and swallow back your own blood, words, and pride? Coward. Are you going to take your anger out on their loved ones? Bitch. What are you going to do? What are you going to do? The moment is disappearing— what is your gut telling you?

uncomfortableuncomfortableuncomfortableuncomfortableun-
comfortableuncomfortableuncomfortableuncomfortableun-
comfortableuncomfortableuncomfortableuncomfortableun-
comfortableuncomfortableuncomfortableuncomfortablehot-
uncomfortableuncomfortableuncomfortableuncomfortableun-
comfortableuncomfortableuncomfortableuncomfortableun-
comfortableuncomfortableuncomfortableuncomfortableun-
comfortableuncomfortableuncomfortableuncomfortableun-
comfortableuncomfortableuncomfortableuncomfortableun-
comfortableuncomfortableuncomfortableuncomfortableun-
comfortableuncomfortableuncomfortableuncomfortableun-
comfortableuncomfortableuncomfortableuncomfortableun-
comfortablehotuncomfortableuncomfortableuncomfort-
ableuncomfortableuncomfortableuncomfortableuncomfort-
ableuncomfortableuncomfortableuncomfortableuncomfort-
ableuncomfortableuncomfortableuncomfortableuncomfort-
ableuncomfortableuncomfortableuncomfortableuncomfort-
ableuncomfortableuncomfortableuncomfortableuncomfort-
ableuncomfortableuncomfortableuncomfortableuncomfort-
ableuncomfortableuncomfortableuncomfortableuncomfort-
ableuncomfortableuncomfortablehotuncomfortableuncom-
fortableuncomfortableuncomfortableuncomfortableuncom-
fortableuncomfortableuncomfortableuncomfortableuncom-
fortableuncomfortableuncomfortableuncomfortableuncom-
fortableuncomfortableuncomfortableuncomfortableuncom-
fortableuncomfortableuncomfortableuncomfortableuncom-
fortableuncomfortableuncomfortableuncomfortableuncom-
fortableuncomfortableuncomfortableuncomfortableuncom-
fortableuncomfortableuncomfortableuncomfortablehotun-
comfortableuncomfortableuncomfortableuncomfortableun-
comfortableuncomfortableuncomfortableuncomfortableun-

comfortableuncomfortableuncomfortableuncomfortableun-
comfortableuncomfortableuncomfortableuncomfortableun-
comfortableuncomfortableuncomfortableuncomfortableun-
comfortableuncomfortableuncomfortableuncomfortableun-
comfortableuncomfortableuncomfortableuncomfortableun-
comfortableuncomfortableuncofortableuncomfortableuncom-
fortableuncomfortableuncomfortableuncomfortableuncom-
fortableuncomfortableuncomfortableuncomfortableuncom-
fortableuncomfortableuncomfortableuncomfortableuncom-
fortableuncomfortableuncomfortableuncomfortableuncom-
fortableuncomfortableuncomfortableuncomfortableuncom-
fortableuncomfortableuncomfortableuncomfortableuncom-
fortableuncomfortableuncomfortableuncomfortableuncom-
fortableuncomfortableuncomfortableuncomfortableuncom-
fortableuncomfortableuncomfortableuncomfortableuncom-
fortableuncomfortableuncomfortableuncomfortableuncom-
fortableuncomfortableuncomfortableuncomfortableuncom-
fortableuncomfortableuncomfortableuncomfortableuncom-
fortableuncomfortableuncomfortableuncomfortableuncom-
fortableuncomfortableuncomfortableuncomfortableuncom-
fortableuncomfortableuncomfortableuncomfortableuncom-
fortableuncomfortableuncomfortableuncomfortableuncom-
fortableuncomfortableuncomfortableuncomfortableuncomfo-
rtableuncomfortableuncomfortableuncomfortableuncomfort-
ableuncomfortableuncomfortableuncomfortableuncomfort-
ableuncomfortableuncomfortableuncomfortableuncomfort-
ableuncomfortableuncomfortableuncomfortableuncomfort-
ableuncomfortableuncomfortableuncomfortableuncomfort-
ableuncomfortableuncomfortableuncomfortableuncomfort-
ableuncomfortableuncomfortableuncomfortableuncomfort-
ableuncomfortableuncomfortableuncomfortableuncomfort-
ableuncomfortableuncomfortableuncomfortableuncomfort-
ableuncomfortableuncomfortableuncomfortable

Hot. Blood boiling. Face flushing. Teeth grinding. Muscles stiffening. Heartbeat quickening. Breath shallowing. Hot. Restless. Uncomfortable.

What are you going to do?

And when it happens, it won't sit with you right. You'll feel a pang in your chest, and you won't be sure if it's anger or sadness. You'll have three options: fight, flight, or—

In the corner of a crowded Thai restaurant, I tell a family friend (an older white woman) that I saw *La La Land* with my friends even though it wasn't very good. She lectures me about how I shouldn't have seen the movie, but instead watched a black movie. She's drunk—we don't know how long she has been drinking today, but she has been driving. I cut into my egg roll, telling her that I had seen all the black films in theaters at that time. Her rebuttal is that I haven't seen all the black films that she believes I should see. I look from my food to her face.

"You know, I have listened to you and your mom, so you need to listen to me, too." Her face is turning red. "I have—me and my sons have—brought you into our home and been there for you graciously. So, you need to do that."

"I have no idea what you're talking about." I pause, her face is red: it could mean incoming tears or fury. "You want me to be gracious?"

And when it happens, it won't sit with you right. You'll feel a pang in your chest, and you won't be sure if it's anger or sadness. You'll have three options: fight, flight, or—

I am at the movie theater with my friend, we are standing in line for concessions. There is another woman of color ordering ahead of us. We stand six feet behind her, like waiting in line to step into the metal detector. A white man hovers behind us with a group of adolescent boys. He gets in our face: "Are you in line?" The woman is still ordering in front of us. We nod. He walks away. A few minutes later, a couple stands behind us, contemplating the menu. The white woman leans her head between us: "Are you two in line?" We look from her, to the woman still ordering.

"Yes, we're just standing an appropriate distance away," I say. She scoffs and turns back to the man with her.

The man with the adolescents returns, "You're in line?"

We stare at him, and the woman ahead of us takes her large popcorn and drink, walking away. When we get into the theater with our snacks and put our 3D glasses on, my friend whispers to me: "Maybe the white people will see us now."

And when it happens, it won't sit with you right. You'll feel a pang in your chest, and you won't be sure if it's anger or sadness. You'll have three options: fight, flight, or—

My pediatrician has been treating me since birth and before me, my older brother. I'm sitting on the paper-covered seat waiting for him to sign off on my physical for softball. He goes over everything with my mother, and my sister waits in the corner, having already gotten her physical. My pediatrician suggests that we get hepatitis vaccines.

"I know that's common where you're from." My over-the-hill, thinning-haired doctor looks down at his clipboard and his glasses slide forward on his nose. My sister, mother, and I all make eye contact and then stare at him.

He must mean Columbus, Ohio.

And when it happens, it won't sit with you right. You'll feel a pang in your chest, and you won't be sure if it's anger or sadness. You'll have three options: fight, flight, or—

I'm in the backseat of my friend's car and we're sitting in traffic on our way to see the holiday lights at the zoo. We've been sitting in traffic for thirty minutes and run out of things to talk about. I stare at the line of unmoving cars in both directions. They start talking about how they both have black friends at school because that's what some white people like to do when they have already bragged about everything else. They describe their black friends with bare minimum details, details that break the stereotypes they know: *he's an engineer, she's pre-med, he's in my fraternity,* or *she's in intervarsity.* The driver stares at me in the rearview mirror with a cheeky grin. I don't want to be here anymore. I don't want to go to the zoo anymore. I don't want to be another one of their tokens.

And when it happens, it won't sit with you right. You'll feel a pang in your chest, and you won't be sure if it's anger or sadness. You'll have three options: fight, flight, or—

My friend and I are discussing blackness: oppression, lack of history, no place. Our brown friend wants to join the conversation, but becomes frustrated when we say it is not his place, he has no authority. He looks at the two of us with a smirk and says: "Raise your hand if you've been to Africa." He puts both hands up.

D'HOMME AMERICAIN

HOW TO EMULATE A WHITE MAN

A **SINGLE SPRITZ,** just before you leave the house. It's difficult to find, as we don't sell it over the counter, but if you can get your hands on a single bottle of D'Homme Americain Eau de Toilette—your life will change. What's in it, you ask? Only the finest ingredients one can procure.

TOP NOTES: BLACK CURRANT, BURNT PINE NEEDLES, BLOOD ORANGE, GRANNY SMITH APPLE, THE DIRT THAT JOHNNY APPLESEED SPIT HIS SEEDS INTO TO FOSTER THE APPLE-PICKING COUNTRY THAT EXISTS IN SOUTH-CENTRAL OHIO, AND JACK DANIEL'S

MIDDLE NOTES: NARCISSUS, WATER HYACINTH, TUBE-ROSE, HONEYSUCKLE, JASMINE, LEATHER, CLARY SAGE, AQUATIC NOTES, SWEAT OF THE FOUNDING FATHERS, INK FROM JOHN HANCOCK'S PEN, AND SPERM FROM THE LAST REMAINING MALE WHITE RHINO

BOTTOM NOTES: MUSK, TOBACCO, ANISE, VANILLA, TONKA BEAN, BLEACH, A SINGLE TEAR FROM ANDREW JACKSON, AND A DROP OF BLOOD FROM AN ENSLAVED PERSON (FOR COLOR)

Shop the collection: California Redwood, Suburban Solitude, Robust Republican, Yankee Doodle, MAGA Ultra, and Heritage

WARNING: D'Homme Americain EDT only provides a feeling, a semblance of the truth. It will not make you invisible to police. It will not move you up to a senior-level position. It will not pay your tuition or offer you a scholarship. It will not bump your credit score. Do not use if part of a minority group. We especially do not recommend use if you are a woman of color.

•

When I say, "American man," we all know who I'm talking about. We all know him, at least one. We met him at the office or in class; he was our college professor, our boss, the worst person in our group project that amounted to 50 percent of our grade. And most likely, he was annoyingly charming, so you would help him with his work or let him get away with minor infractions against your brain, your body, your existence. I don't want to say this, but I guess it's only true: In a way, we made the American man who he is today.

There's a deep-rooted shame in that, I think, but it's too early to say.

Maybe, like me, you loved these men. These white men who took up so much space in my daily life that I didn't know black people could exist without encountering white people—or the opposite, that white people could exist without encountering black people—that people could exist without acknowledging another race. Growing up, that's something I didn't notice because I didn't live it. I was constantly engaging with people from different cultures than mine, and I was constantly existing as one of few people of color in a space. In a way, I guess that made me the disruption in the lives of the white people I grew up with—the anomaly, the speck of pepper in a pile of salt, the difference, the oddball. But kids understand race differently. Racism is not inherent but inherited in the home. Parents telling children things about the other children: she's poor, she's ghetto, she's dirty, she's not like you, she's not as smart as you, you need to be her friend, don't talk to her, don't touch her, she's not one of us. And then children come to school and say it to your face, as if you knew all along—as if you couldn't not know all along.

As it happens now, most of the white men I grew up with, liked, loved, etc. when I was younger are existing elsewhere and have hopefully forgotten me. Though, I've found that I am hard to forget for some reason; invisibility requires effort from me. If one of you are reading this . . . I guess, good for you? Welcome? This essay isn't really for you, but it is dedicated to you. I think about these white boys, now men, a lot lately, because the more time that passes from the last time that I saw them, the more I realize how much time I spent catering to them. There's a photo of me spending reading time in kindergarten reading to a white boy. There were the ones who pulled my hair. The one who wouldn't tell me he liked me back. The one who left me at homecoming. The one who left me at prom. The one who abandoned his best friend for me. The one I abandoned all my friends for. The one who lapped me in gym and jogged backwards to motivate me to run faster. The one who knocked my Beanie Baby off my desk. The one who copied off my homework. The one I tutored in French. The ones whose college essays I spent my lunchtime heavily editing with pink pen. The ones who told me why I got into college (affirmative action, apparently). The ones who wanted to date my friends. The ones who wanted to fuck my friends. The ones who slept on my chest or in my lap. The one who beat me with a belt on the bus a couple times. The ones who made me cry in the locker room, the bathroom, my bedroom. The ones who I wrote poems about and filled composition notebooks with. The one who ghosted me because I looked "too happy" in our photos. The one who told me to kill myself. The one I thought about killing myself for. The one who sent me fake Valentine's carnations. The one who asked me why I stopped liking him—

Honestly, the white boys I knew in middle and high school did the most damage, but they also taught me the most about where I fit in their world. How many times can you tell a white man no? Three times. The first, he'll laugh because he won't believe you. The second, he will ask, "Really?" And the third, he will remind you of everything he's ever done for you.

Instead of saying no a fourth time, look at his face for what may be the last time and remember that moment, because for him that will be your blackest moment, that will be the moment where your relationship splinters and the color drains from the room—relish it.

I'm trying my hardest to keep this essay from becoming a tangent, to prove that I am not scorned by the American male because I'm not, I simply know who he is. I know that his existence is determined by mine. That is how hierarchy works. That is how American men don't have to climb the same ladder to success as me because they emerge from the womb being lifted by the hands of others to the top. And we all know who I'm talking about: the American men with the diamond-studded spoon in their mouths, with mothers who spend every moment reaffirming that they are the most important, the only thing that matters, and these are words they will hear for the rest of their lives from teachers, coaches, employers, bosses, and everyone else. Even I am guilty of helping white men to achieve more than me, wasting my time and energy to help them for a meager "thank you" as they make their way to the top and I till away at the bottom attempting to create a legacy for myself.

In many ways, I was conditioned to aspire to be the American male. As if he's doing something groundbreaking by being born into privilege and wealth. And after spending half of my life at this point pandering, loving, and chipping away at my self to make these men feel better about themselves, I've decided that I don't want to be anything like them. There's nothing that a white American man has that I want. Of course, money, privilege, and power are all things that I need to taste even a simulacrum of the American dream—but there have to be other ways to earn those three things rather than becoming just like him.

There's the difference between me and him: He was born with it, and I have to work for it.

Maybe he's born with it, maybe it's white privilege.

I watched live video footage of white men storming the Capitol. Paralyzed by fear on my couch, I watched them climb the walls, break through glass windows, and force their way into one of the most secure buildings in the nation. I watched, and I waited. I watched as a temper tantrum escalated and transformed into terrorism. I watched as the same police who terrorized our streets this past summer with rubber bullets and pepper spray, with curfews and riot gear, did nothing.

No rubber bullets. No violence. No justice. No peace.

Oh, to be a white man in America—your president loved you.

We'll all tell different stories to our children. Mine will be of fury. Mine will be a reckoning. Mine will be told against the melody of my sister's cries of pain after she was thrown to the ground by a police officer, who snatched off her goggles and sprayed mace directly in her face. She was a legal observer. The harmony will be the simultaneous hum of cell phones ringing with the emergency alert of a citywide curfew.

We'll tell ghost stories about him under moonlight.

A LIBERATED
BLACK BEAUTY

If you could live at any time, which would you pick?

I **WAS ALWAYS PRACTICAL:** answering with the '90s or '60s, while my friends imagined living during Elizabethan, Ancient Greek, and Roman eras. I envied their privilege of being able to imagine themselves in any known time of the world and existing peacefully. But, as a black girl, I knew that if I didn't want to be a slave, then my options were limited to Ancient and pre-colonial Africa and the twentieth century, which was still volatile, but at least I'd be free.

In truth, I wanted to be a woman in the 1920s: the jazz era, the world of flappers, the Harlem Renaissance. When I was in tenth grade, we read and analyzed *The Great Gatsby* until we knew everything about it—from what each mention of the colors green and white meant, to flipping the book upside down to analyze the cover—and I grew to love the book, although it didn't seem like it was for me, lacking characters who looked like me or were even poor like me. But there is a brief scene when all the main white characters are driving into the city, and they pass a car full of black people celebrating as a white man chauffeurs them to their destination. It's the only section in the entire novel that portrays black people in a positive light, and really, the only scene I remember about black people. It was rare to read about black characters free from suffering and stereotypes, and I wanted to be one of those wealthy black people. I craved their freedom to celebrate and do as they please. And while these characters didn't mean too much in the entirety of the book, I've never forgotten them and their chauffeur driving them out of town.

I didn't know much about the '20s until college. I took a theater class on Advanced Makeup Application and Design, and our first assignment was to create period looks. I was assigned the 1920s, probably because I was the only black student in the class and the history of beauty and makeup tends to ignore the narratives and beauty of people of color, even though it ultimately tracks back to Ancient Egyptians and Persians, but I digress. The rest of my class was assigned periods from colorless times when paleness was desired to the point of painting one's face with lead paint. But beauty in the 1920s was revolutionary; the nation was at a moment in American history when makeup was no longer a mark for promiscuous women, but for all women. It was a moment that introduced timeless beauty trends: the rouge cupid's bow lip, eyes darkened with kohl liner to create a sultry smolder, and intense blush applied to the apples of the cheeks. Women wore cropped hair; their legs were visible, and maybe their thighs in the right minidress. I fell down a rabbit hole on the internet searching 1920s fashion and beauty trends for hours. Then I went to class, painting my face with my Ben Nye kit according to a carefully drawn sketch I'd created. I was still new to makeup, so I didn't blend my Adobe Brown highlighter with my Midnite Brown shadow very well. But, as researched, I applied my Flame Red dry rouge onto the apples of my cheeks in a perfect semicircle, lined my eyes with the black eye pencil in my kit, and used to it fill my already thick brows. The final touch was the coat of Boysenberry crème color on my lips. The overall look wasn't perfect, but I put on a pair of pearl earrings, wiped my muddled makeup-covered hands on my smock and walked out under the blinding stage lights for my evaluation.

I have this fantasy of being Daisy Buchanan in *The Great Gatsby*, specifically when she's lying on the couch in her sunroom in all white; and the doors and windows to the room are open, so the white curtains are billowing, and this moment of serenity is interrupted by Nick when he enters the room, but Daisy doesn't care, because Daisy has no worries, beyond Gatsby. The contrast of the color white on brown and black skin would make this scene much more aesthetically pleasing to me, because black people look great in white, but there would be this ominous undertone of being consumed by the whiteness of the room. I've seen only a few movies that positively portray black women in the 1920s. I have seen *Chicago*, with Queen Latifah in a supporting role as Matron Mama Morton: big, bold, black, and beautiful. She's the warden of the jail throughout the film. There is *The Color Purple*, the most honest portrayal: both positive and negative, thoroughly exploring Alice Walker's definition of "womanism" throughout the film. And, most recently, there is Disney's *The Princess and The Frog*, about Tiana, a waitress turned into a frog transformed into a princess who owns her own restaurant. And even though Tiana's conservative yellow ankle-length dress and tied-back hair exist as a complete opposite to Shug Avery and Matron Mama Morton's bodies draped in low-cut dresses covered with crystals, sequins, and pearls, and their fabulous headdresses to accentuate their cropped haircuts, she is still a strong representation of an everyday, hardworking, goal-driven young black woman in the 1920s. These black women were nothing like Daisy Buchanan lounging in all white. But still, I admired their ability to be so beautiful and happy in the '20s, singing and dancing, working and dreaming, while remaining honest and humbled.

In the 1920s, women began embracing their bodies and leaving the house, drifting away from mundane, silent domestic roles. No longer woman: the object, the personal property; but woman: the worker, the voter, the liberated. And the 1920s wasn't just momentous for women, but also for black people, who were making an exodus from the south to the north, migrating and exposing the world to their culture in urban areas like Chicago, Philly, Cleveland, and Harlem. The black body had been freed and the black world burst with art and music, words and movement, fellowship and history—a renaissance to behold. Let me return to that scene in *The Great Gatsby*, this time in the 2013 film: black men and women dancing in the back of their car, dressed up in gold, white, and turquoise, pouring champagne, clinking glasses, all while their white driver takes them out of the city. A scene less than a minute a long, but so crucial to the film that it is slowed down while the narrator passes the scene to emphasize the power of the black people in the car as one of the women casually reaches towards the front to snap at their driver for more champagne.

While the black perspective of the 1920s is limited in media, there are enough books by black authors and glimpses in movies to put together a cohesive image of the renaissance. And of course, in the fictional world, the stressors of war and racism are pushed to the background for stories of the mundane and for character development. I imagine that, as a black female writer, I would have easily merged into the scene, sitting in the back of coffeehouses and clubs engaging in friendly debates with other writers over our work, politics, and ideas. I could have understood jazz the way the generations before me do, feeling the emotion of each note. I would have enjoyed feeling strands of pearls rolling on my skin while indulging in the ferocity of the twenties. I would have spent my days writing for freedom and my nights dancing freely in the dark. The 1920s, when black voices were rising from the earth, when freedom was pumping in the veins of chocolate- and honey-toned skin, and they called themselves the New Negro.

Gaining on a century later, black culture is no longer in its renaissance, but in a movement more akin to a revolution. The black voice and black body are attempting to break the sound barrier, desperate to be heard. Generations later, and we are still fighting for the acknowledgment of our existence as humans. Beauty is inherent in all of that. Black beauty is political. Dark skin, full lips, voluptuous and curved frames, and naturally curly and kinky hair have been mocked and parodied for centuries, but now they are craved by white bodies, implanted and modified under white skin. Black bodies, just like beauty, have become a trend. My body has been a fetish. My body has been craved, ridiculed, disregarded, and denied. But this is still my body, this is still my skin.

When I started to wear makeup, I followed the style of the 1920s. I had my striking red lip courtesy of MAC Cosmetics, and I had my Sephora blush and eyeliners. The perk of having a vintage style in the twenty-first century is the opportunity to modernize. The perk of wearing makeup as black woman in the twenty-first century is abundance of colors and palettes to choose from. I don't get dolled up very often, but when I do, I tend to go all out and emulate that liberated, artistic woman of the 1920s: I like to show off my legs in customized vintage dresses, I push back my afro, put it in an updo, or let shrinkage have its way; and I love to dance, to close my eyes and follow the rhythm with my body. I do not blend my concealer or line my lips thinking about others' politics. Makeup-wise, I have my 1920s staple blush, no longer simply on the apples of my cheeks, but riding the contoured line of my cheekbones; I still rock the dark eyeliner in appropriate shades of metallic green and black, and my rouge lip has evolved from only matte reds to including hot pink, royal blue, deep purple, black, and deep brown (nude). And I'm hoping that soon, I can be bold like those women in the 1920s were bold in their writing and marching and dancing and lives, not just with embracing my own beauty, but also in my own work.

BODIES OF WATER

YOU KNOW, they say black girls don't swim.

The first rule is to hold your breath.

Who decided to wade into the water first? Was it clear, no surprises at the bottom, nothing to fear? Could she see her future in her reflection—that she would resurface and return to land?

I've been swimming since I was a kid. I had one of those baby pools, about a foot deep. There are photos of toddler-me—pink bikini-clad and baby afro transforming into dreadlocks—standing in my pool on the porch, splashing and laughing.

There is something refreshing about water, as if it's where I belong.

Swim instructors teach little kids the basics: hold your breath underwater, blow bubbles, kick your feet, float on your back. They put their arms underneath our bodies to hold us up until we learn to do it ourselves. What should be a breath sounds like a gasp as we hold onto the concrete ledge, half submerged in water, legs thrashing.

Float on your back.   Hold your breath.   Don't forget to breathe.

If you think about it, they're teaching us how to survive.

The swimming pool is never filled with black bodies. You're thinking of the ocean.

Underwater, we open our eyes. The chlorine burns, but we want to see what it looks like below. Blurry brown limbs. Everything else is bright blue and white. There is no sound except our own.

At a Girl Scouts pool party, I cross over to the deep end to talk to a friend. I lose my grip and suddenly, water is more everywhere than it was before. Am I screaming? I am thrashing. This is my life—I am too young to die, too young to be swallowed. One of the mothers dives into the pool to save me, cell phone still in her pocket.

First rule of drowning: Don't panic, or you'll only sink faster.

We go to the waterpark every weekend in the summers. On the way there, we sit in the trunk of the station wagon waving at cars in our bathing suits. We cascade down waterslides, float and fuss in the Lazy River, and watch movies in the wave pool on Saturday nights. We bake in the sun and cool off in the water. Water runs down our legs as we explore the park. When the bell tolls, we stand crowded together waiting for the bucket to pelt us with gallons of water.

Someone pops open the fire hydrant on the corner, but we don't run through it. We watch it gush into the street and recycle into the sewer until there's barely any left.

In the wave pool, I swim back to the shore from the deep end. I dive underwater to see how far I can get and when I resurface, a wave knocks me back under before I can catch my breath. I try again and am forced back down, closer to the shallows. Once more, the water knocks me down, and I am drowning between the dozens of bodies riding the waves. My swimsuit catches on the jagged surface of the concrete—I sit in the shallows, coughing, finally able to catch my breath.

One day, we become too old for the children's area at the waterpark. We hear the bell toll while standing in line for the waterslides. We count down the seconds to when the water will fall.

I never learned if my father knew how to swim.

In high school, as a camp counselor, I must pass the "lifeguard test" to swim in the deep. This pool is warm, filled with young white bodies that I am supposed to keep from drowning. The test: swim from the shallow end to the deep end without stopping and tread water for two minutes. It is a crooked line, but I freestyle swim from one end to the other. Out of breath, I bicycle kick until the other counselor says I can stop. The kids are splashing in the shallows, no one actually learns how to swim—they hold onto the edges before letting go for the thrill of it.

My friends put makeup on before they get in the pool. They sit in the shallows and on the edge of the pool talking about boys. I am at the opposite end, treading water and diving, trying to touch the bottom.

A true scenario: my white friends screaming at the kinks of my hair floating on the surface. I have contaminated the pool with my blackness. They cup the water and my hair in their hands and toss it from the pool like drowning insects.

An imagined scenario: I am caught in the wet strands of their hair like prey.

Black people can't swim, but if they do, throw acid in the pool.

In the Midwest, we have creeks, rivers, and lakes. I spend much of my childhood hunting for crayfish in creeks and navigating shallow, murky bodies of water. In Chicago, it takes me an entire summer before I actually swim in Lake Michigan—a black body treading in the dark.

I don't like the ocean. I stand at its edge and hear its secrets in the swell.

Water signs in Mars, Venus, and Pluto: Cancer/Cancer/Scorpio. As a fire sign, my watery influences are reason for shame. Water is too emotional, too sensitive, too flexible, too guarded. Fire and water do nothing but create steam.

Water is a feminine element. My mother is a Pisces. My best friend. A boy I thought I loved. So much water and yet, never enough.

Water doesn't actually put out fires. The proper thing to do is smother it.

When my mother is baptized, she wears a large t-shirt from my middle school engineering camp. A white man preaches as he dips her dry body into a pool and she resurfaces, drenched and searching. He says something about giving everything up to Jesus. And I wonder: everything, even my pride? One by one, I watch them wade into the pool, dip, and resurface—clean slates.

Black people and water are usually allegories for the Middle Passage.

When we took the campers tubing, I would have to get out of the raft and pull them down the river in the shallow spots. Sometimes, I would be walking and hit a drop zone, falling below the surface, out of view. That's what the lifejackets were for—I'd pop back up, sputtering and treading water.

At the end of Beyoncé's "Formation" music video she lay on a police car and they are both swallowed by the water. Someone says, *Golly! Look at that water boy, oh Lord!*

You know how many people of color have been devoured by the current?

The water is never just right. It is always too warm/too hot/too cold, and the only way to acclimate is to suffer.

Scald your wrist reaching the shower knob to point it an inch to the left. Slip further into the hot tub until your brain believes you're comfortable.

When it is cold, it is a process: Wade until the water meets your thighs, pause. Wade until it meets your waist and spread your legs to drench the warmest part of you. Splash your chest and stomach until everything is wet. Wade up to your underboob, take a breath, and sink.

They ask me, you know how to swim? Of course.

This essay is an allegory, but also an ode—the glass of water on your nightstand.

I realized I was afraid of open water right before I turned fourteen. In Michigan, our boat tipped, and I found myself hanging upside down from the sail with my foot caught in a rope. We floated in the water waiting for rescue, and the sky had darkened dramatically. Something was in the water with us: Pike? Mermaids? Souls?

When Ariel trades her voice for legs, she finds out what it means to drown.

Never been baptized. Forgot to dip my hands in the holy water the one time I went to mass.

There is that scene in *Amistad* when the African woman steps off the deck of the boat with her baby and disappears into the current.

When I get stoned and swim, I forget to breathe. I stay underneath the water where it's quiet and undisturbed until I remember that I need air. I quit getting high around bodies of water; I was too eager to be consumed by it.

Don't be alarmed—I am only floating on my stomach. I am not a corpse; every now and then I gasp and sputter for air.

I've never swam in the ocean.

Black girls can't swim—afraid to get their hair wet.

Floating is all about body fat. It's also about trust and not being afraid of silence.

I keep thinking about black bodies in water, my body in water, and why it feels like I am missing.

We know nothing about how deep the ocean goes; what happens in the dark.

I prefer the deep end because if you can stay underwater for long enough, you begin to decipher the white noise. Sometimes I pray down there—for silence, for solitude, for life.

Now, I wear ear plugs in the water. I mold silicone into the shape of my ear canal, rolling it onto the skin so it seals. Everything underwater is white noise and shadows.

And here, I'll sound like a broken record when I tell you to believe that water is a hallowed ground. A last reminder to the body that the earth reclaims itself—imagine all that pressure, grinding bones to sand.

You know how to survive? Of course.

NINE MINUTES

<u>GATHER DNA</u>

*DO **NOT** EAT, DRINK, SMOKE, OR CHEW GUM FOR **30
MINUTES** BEFORE GIVING YOUR SALIVA SAMPLE.*

*FILL THE TUBE WITH SALIVA TO THE BLACK
WAVY LINE.*

11:48 P.M.—I'm watching *The Office* with the tube at my lips, filling my mouth with saliva and letting it dribble into the plastic container. It's a Tuesday night in Chicago, and I am finally preparing my sample for AncestryDNA. I've wanted to take a DNA test for a few years, hoping to find out more about my father's background and his family—answers to questions I didn't have time to ask before he died—about my heritage, my enslaved ancestors, but I have doubts.

Half of AncestryDNA's map of Africa (Chad, Mauritania, Niger, Sudan, Ethiopia, Eritrea, and Somalia) is not included in the options for ancestry results. *Somehow*, they have not acquired enough saliva samples from people in these areas. If I have any Saharan African roots, how will I know? The researchers would categorize me as "Other/Unknown." My mouth is dry, so I struggle to produce the sample quickly, taking at least four minutes to get the bubbles above the line. It seems impossible that my spit can define me. Online, I check the boxes that say I do not want to meet any potential relatives. There is only one thing I want: the map, the list of countries and regions that make up my ethnicity, my blackness.

REPLACE THE FUNNEL WITH THE CAP. TIGHTEN TO RELEASE STABILIZING FLUID.

11:53 P.M.—It wasn't until after our father died that my sister and I started asking our mother where we come from. At our private school in Ohio, we had been assigned an abnormal amount of heritage homework and projects: Where are you from? Interview a grandparent; interview someone who grew up during WWII. What does your name mean? Where did your family immigrate from?

And for most of these questions, we didn't have answers. My sister interviewed our grandmother and tried to adopt our great-grandmother's name as a second middle name. I interviewed my seventh-grade history teacher about "counterculture" and Woodstock. Our family did not immigrate from anywhere—we had no Ellis Island stories to share with the classroom. What we knew was Ohio and Louisiana, very little about the latter, but Ohio had been our family's home for generations, which made us black, and only black.

For a long time, we were the only black girls in our classes, which didn't mean much when we were eight, but by sixteen we were hyper aware of it. Black bodies in white classrooms always seem out of place—students staring at me while we read *To Kill a Mockingbird* aloud or watched Civil War videos, as if they were waiting for me to divulge exclusive information from my inherited fountain of blackness—as if my skin alone would offer the answers they sought.

Everything I knew about blackness I learned at home or in books. In second grade, we studied the entire United States, learning their histories and state symbols. I was assigned Kentucky, the Bluegrass State, and neighbor to my beloved Ohio, sharing cardinals and mountains. Kentucky is the only reason I know how to spot a dogwood tree. In third grade, we studied Europe and Australia—I quickly came to know more about Aborigines and Iceland than I did about slavery and Martin Luther King Jr. Finally, when I was nine, we learned about Native Americans and black people because we were planted in Columbus, Ohio. Ohio being an Indigenous word and previously populated by several Indigenous tribes, we took field trips to burial mounds, Native American cemeteries, and caves throughout central Ohio. And there is Ohio's history as a free state: the river existing as a border to freedom, images of white women hanging quilts in their windows at night—we learned about "Johnny Cake," Harriet Tubman, and "drinking gourds."

Once, a white girl brought in "Johnny Cake" as a treat for all of us, displaying her fourth-grade understanding of slavery and blackness—it didn't taste like home and crumbled in my hand. I'm sure she made it from scratch, using cornmeal and no sugar, instead of buying a fifty-cent box of Jiffy mix. The slave experience versus the black experience. I remember one traumatizing field trip, where we simulated a "slave run," my palms and knees digging into rocks and dirt as me and my classmates hid underneath the floor of a cabin; a classmate "caught" and several others shoved into a cage made of chicken wire.

DNA tests are most profitable in the United States, a country built on imperialism and immigration. A place where "white" and "black" exist as identities. My high school history teacher made sure to let all the white students know that they were not "Caucasian," that their families did not originate in the Caucasus Mountains, that they were only white. She didn't need to tell me that I was only black. Blackness is a construct morphed into an identity, the same way white people appropriated the term "American" to mean people in the United States, excluding Canada, Mexico, Central America, South America, and the Caribbean. But my body screams black: wide hips, wide nose, dark skin, and kinky, black hair. The answers that I've been looking for are in my flesh, my genetic code—but I'm still not sure I can articulate my questions.

SHAKE THE TUBE FOR AT LEAST FIVE SECONDS.

11:54 P.M.—My mother told stories that we were Haitian, which was exciting because before being Haitian, we had only been black. Black as in erasure. Black as in our ancestry could only be mapped to where our parents were born. Black as in nowhere. And being Haitian seemed probable; I was a sun child, spending all the time I could basking in the sunshine, letting the melanin in my cells bake to a crisp. I called myself a coffee bean. But I was language-less, culture-less; everything I knew about Haiti was from a textbook.

Turns out, I was not Haitian. Back to black. Black as in nothing. Black as in consuming.

When I was twelve, I decided I was Creole. My father was from Louisiana, and his mother was biracial. I understood that Creole people were mixed people in or from Louisiana, which made my father a version of Creole. So, I was Creole until a boy asked me what kind of Creole I was—I didn't know what to say, and he laughed at me. He was Creole; I wasn't anymore. Again, I was "I don't know." Once again, I was black. "Just black," I told anyone who asked. The black face in the classroom; the black body in the locker room.

There is a beauty mark on my left index finger, and for the longest time I thought it was a splinter; it just appeared. I've never found myself beautiful, but the beauty marks keep appearing all over my body: my arms, my breasts, my thighs— no one's ever called me beautiful. I hold the tube carefully between two fingers: What does it mean to be black? The saliva sample is an eight ball: Ask again later.

PLACE THE TUBE IN THE COLLECTION BAG.

11:56 P.M.—Over the years, I have been embracing my "just" blackness more. There is satisfaction in not having to list all the different ways I am "exotic," there is something special in just being another random black spatter in a Pollack. In college, race became something always at the forefront of my mind. Maybe because I lived in the south. Maybe because I was surrounded by wealthy white people who didn't know any black people. Maybe because of our lack of shared experiences. Maybe because black people started being killed more visibly. Then I had to think about my future and my present, and I had to reconsider the privileges of my past. One day, I woke up and there was a dead black boy on the internet, lying cold in the summer heat. Another day, there was a new barrier between me and my childhood friends—my blackness finally visible.

White spaces will blur you to the point where you don't consider race anymore, you're colorless, you're molecules, invisible to the eye. I became obsessed with that invisibility, which at any time could flip to hypervisibility—all eyes on me—at any moment. I googled my blackness, began reading up on the histories of black men and women, watching documentaries, and having these conversations with my black friends.

After the non-indictment of Darren Wilson, for which my friends and I watched Ferguson on fire from our living room, our college had a meeting for black people to gather in solidarity and discuss our presence on campus in the midst of racial tensions. We were 6 percent of the student body. The next day there was a meeting for the entire campus to discuss the same microaggressions and tensions. My white friend attended and returned to the house distraught, but also angry that we, her three black friends, had not gone with her. She tried to tell us about how black people were being treated in the United States as if we didn't know. We laughed at her frustration, shrugged our shoulders, and turned back around to do our homework.

In my college psychology classes, we were forced to fill out The Holmes and Rahe Stress Scale because we were college students: overwhelmed and stressed, meat in a pressure cooker. Present-day Chicago, I fill out the scale again. I circle "YES" on question #5, "death of close family member." Sixty-three points, just for that. My score is 455 out of 600. The lower the score the better. The test says I have a high risk of becoming ill soon. I knock on wood. I am already sick of the world, every single day. The test doesn't know that. The test doesn't know I am seeking out my family history—how many points is that? The test doesn't know that I've been starving myself, that I've isolated myself from my friends because I have no idea what will happen when I lose the security of school, that I feel my future unraveling, that I do not want to leave my house due to all this imagined shame and expectations. The test doesn't know that stress is the only way I know how to feel normal anymore. The symptoms of the United States are embedded in my body, dormant in my code, coating my tongue.

SEAL THE BAG WITH ADHESIVE STRIP. PLACE YOUR SAMPLE IN THE PREPAID MAILING BOX.

11:57 P.M.—This particular DNA test costs $100, but I got mine on sale. I decided to take the plunge after my creative writing professor encouraged me to find out more about my father for an essay I'd written about his house, and in doing so, myself. But I was interested in both sides of my family, specifically how far back I could go. Could I find the plantations? Could I find the boats?

At nineteen, I visited a plantation in North Carolina. Next to the hog pen was a small log cabin: dirt floor, two cots, a ladder leading to the second floor. A sign on the cabin listed the names of the thirty-six slaves who lived there. I stood in the cabin alone—it was my first plantation. I had known, logically, that slavery happened, and that at least one of the white families I'd grown up with had, at one point, probably owned slaves. But I didn't feel the weight of the past until I stood in that room. A map could only tell me the where and maybe the when of my ancestors, but what I needed to learn and understand was *how*. How did my ancestors survive and what did hope look like to them—a generation that only imagined freedom?

The DNA kit is smaller than I anticipated. I expected a booklet and a map—instead I got a tube and a pre-addressed box. I expected to receive a hard-copy version of my results— instead I had to register online. DNA and genetic ancestry tests are marketed to a white audience: They can afford it, and the tests will reveal trace amounts of unknown ethnicity in their DNA. In the commercials, a man trades in his lederhosen for a kilt because he is not German, but Scottish; a woman walks around various ceramic pots with Indigenous designs. There are no black people in the commercials.

But there is nothing more important to blackness and black culture than heritage. Why else does my family have all these photos, notes, and memorabilia? There is a reason I try to record every single thing I do, be it a written history, a video, or a photograph; a reason storytelling feels so natural and important to my being. This recording and collecting counters the active erasure happening to blackness and black people— it reminds people of the true size of Africa on the maps, of her diverse countries; it tells the stories of overcrowded boats and bloodied crops; and we have photos and videos so that we don't end up lost in life, inhabiting a nowhere for forgotten people and their cultures.

MAIL IN YOUR SAMPLE.

NEXT MORNING, 8:45 A.M.—I am going home, flying back to Ohio from Chicago for a three-week mini-vacation. The small white box with my saliva sample is packed in my duffle bag. I have slight anxiety at its existence, at what will happen in two months when I receive my ethnicity map. Finally, I can find out these answers, and begin remapping my family tree, retelling their stories, and understanding the histories that assembled to produce me. I am assigning myself the role of recorder and anthropologist. I am already thinking about when I should take another DNA test from another company to compare the results. I am wondering if once I have the results, I should travel to these places around the world, or whether I start with the United States and map my ancestors' paths backwards from Ohio.

I want to be in the physical spaces: I want to see the houses, to walk through the fields, to explore the migration. I can only imagine the stories of what happened over the Atlantic, the void between a continent and her people—the emptiness of the Atlantic, the bodies floating and then sinking to the bottom. The deeper I go underwater when swimming, the quieter it gets—is that what it feels like in the void? I am afraid of the ocean and its secrets. I only stand in the shallows, staring at the water's change in color as it swells in front of me. The bodies trapped 8,486 meters below the surface by the pressure of the water—if they're still there it'd be impossible to tell they're African. They'd be nothing more than bleached skeletons, crumbling into the sand.

And of course, there is the fear of being not black enough, of being too white, too other, too non-black. I know I am black, but can you tell me if I'm African? Can you tell me who my ancestors were before they were enslaved? Race is a construct, blackness is a construct, black culture is man-made, handcrafted. It's only when faced with non-black people in non-black cultures that blackness becomes a smudge, a choice—a burden, an attack, an act of violence.

Maybe I should burn the evidence before it gets into the wrong hands. The DNA test results will have read my palms, but can only tell me about my past—what about my future? No matter the results, I'll always be black: phenotypically, culturally, and psychologically black. Blackness goes deeper than skin cells. When I am buying elbow macaroni and five different types of expensive cheese at the grocery store, I am still black. When I am swimming in a pool with chlorine bleaching my dyed curls, I am still black. When I walk into a room or a space that I am not expected to be in, I am my most authentic, unapologetic black. No DNA results can change that. I drop my sample into the mailbox. Pick-up is at 11:15 A.M.

YOUR TEST WILL BE COMPLETED 6–8 WEEKS
FROM THE TIME WE RECEIVE YOUR SAMPLE.

MARGINALIA

Black (adj.): (1) of the very darkest color owing to the absence or complete absorption of light; the opposite of white; (2) of any human group having dark colored skin, especially of African or Australian Aboriginal ancestry; (3) (of a period of time or situation) characterized by tragic or disastrous events; causing despair or pessimism

I am not a:

☐ STRAIGHT   ☐ CIS-   ☐ WHITE   ☐ MAN

What I am, is a:

☐ STRAIGHT   ☐ CIS-   ☐ BLACK   ☐ WOMAN

But don't you want to be a white man? Don't you want to walk into a room and know that everyone will see and hear you? Don't you want that?

I feel like . . . we're forgetting about the multiplicity of white men. The term "white men" has generalized them into this Wrigleyville roaming, fratty type of bro—not the nerds or the poor, the farmers, the coal miners, the racists, the good ol' boys, and the rest of them. The "it" white man right now is Casey Affleck, I think. He's the one to beat. I spend way too much of my time thinking about white men.

A(n) (abandoned) dating profile:

Looking for a "Help Her Whitey"
    24, Chicago, IL
    Must be a straight, cis-white man of moderate wealth between the ages of 26 and 40 that is currently on a career path to a business-related CEO or prominent field in the sciences. No kids.

"Help Her Whitey" was described by a professor of color as a white man or woman who tags along with a person of color throughout their day, so that when they need to interact with white people, the white man (or woman) can speak for the person of color. My professor saw this on television, and she thought it was funny. I found it funny. Some of my white peers shifted uncomfortably, others chuckled.

But during break, a white girl asked me if I had a "Help Her Whitey." And there was a break in my code, a jumble of letters—

or maybe it was a line break, when I thought: What kind of mark would my hand leave on her face? Would it redden immediately, swell up; would my nails catch on the ghostly pale skin of her cheek and leave three red lines traveling downwards from the rise of her mediocre cheekbones?

—the code fixed itself. "No." I shrugged. "I don't need one."

Would I marry a white man? Absolutely, but he must stand two steps behind me in photos.

I am all too aware of the way power is (not) shared in these United States of America. I am aware that if there is a white man with me, he is expected to provide any and all answers. I am aware that if there is a white man with me, I am not expected to speak. That if there is a white man with me, I'm more likely to offend. That I am more likely to be regressed into a primitive archetype: the woman from Joseph Conrad's *Heart of Darkness*, wailing in the riverbed, absent of her previous strength; Jezebel; the help; a mammy; an accessory.

It's not only white men, but men in general. I will end up someone's wife. I will end up someone's employee. I will end up someone's something. She is his ____. She is my ____. This is my ____. That is his ____.

My neighbor is drunk one afternoon and asks me to sit with her while I eat my Wendy's. I tell her I'm reading Elizabeth Alexander's *The Black Interior* and that sometimes I write about race. She tells me that "black people don't have it that bad." *I'm First Nation*, she says, *Trail of Tears. I'm First Nation, do you know what that means?*

Why do people compare atrocities? Should we measure the amount of blood spilled, the amount of blood in the fertilizer as we trace the footsteps of our ancestors? This entire country is hallowed ground.

As a kid, I watched the other children run up and down Ohio burial mounds.

How is a mass grave dug? How many bodies should it fit? How many bodies are forced to fit? How do you deposit body after body without covering it up? When does a corpse become a body and a body become a corpse—what is the difference? When do people begin to use the word "genocide"?

I don't want to lose you, reader. Please do not settle into the lilt of language, into the stories, into the imagery. Do you know why I have to write this? Do you know why I have to use my time to tell you this? Can you guess how they tried to break me? Are you one of them? Do you want to be?

In the United States of America, a boy becomes a man based on the color of his skin, not his age. In this country, it's fine to kill a black boy because a black boy eventually grows into a black man, and a black man is someone who should be stopped at all costs—be it his life or his freedom.

Sometimes, I find myself in the middle of doing something and I freeze, as if time has stopped, and I press a hand to my belly, overcome with dread. And in that time—a few seconds or minutes of me standing, mid-action—I imagine the life and death of my son. I imagine bringing him home and cradling him. I imagine sending him off to school for the first time. I imagine telling him what to fear, how to behave. I imagine losing him at the hands of an afraid or angry white man. I imagine making the funeral plans. I imagine disappearing, inconsolable. And then I am unfrozen, returning to the space I am currently in, feeling sick, lamenting the life of a boy who does not exist, may not ever exist.

This feeling happens often. And the boy does exist, he's just not mine, and I am terrified for the day that changes.

I can see the anxiety rising from your toes. I can see the way your Adam's apple jumps when we make eye contact. You avert your gaze when I catch you looking—those few disoriented blinks when our eyes meet. What are you thinking about when you look at me? Do you think I shouldn't be able to navigate this space so surely, with such confidence?

True story: I'm at Jackson's house one summer—there are three of us. Once again, I am the only black person in the room. I'm sitting at the kitchen table, talking to Greg who is chopping something—vegetables, fruit? Jackson walks up behind him and places his hands around his eyes. Taken by surprise, Greg stops chopping and spits: *Don't be such a nigger.* And I can't remember if my mouth fell open with that small *pop* sound, but I remember my eyes widening as Jackson removed his hands, and they both looked at me, waiting for a reaction. But I didn't say anything, my heart doing that skip it does whenever I hear the word "nigger" slip from anyone's mouth with ease.

The one with the knife: *Oh no! Please don't cut me! Don't cut me!*

Greg put both hands up defensively, still holding the knife. And he laughed. They both laughed. And I stared at the knife in his hands and my hands flat on the table, and I didn't understand how I had become the aggressor—how I was both victim and aggressor when the knife was in his hand and he could have held it up to my neck, called me a nigger, and made me realize our entire friendship was a farce.

Don't be such a nigger.

How?

noun *offensive*: a contemptuous term for a black or dark-skinned person.

(Spanish) negro › (French) nègre › (English) neger ›

› nigger (late 17th century)

(English) Negro ›

They (you) may say that she is (I am):

aggressive   angry   violent   savage   evil   sassy
loud   intimidating   a bitch   an angry black woman

I have always been perceived as different when people talk demographics. When they talk about young people, I am different because I act older / wise / [insert word]. When they talk about women, I am different because I am cool / down to earth / [insert word]. When they talk about black people, I am different because I am calm / "not black" / [insert word].

I am "not black" because I am an "Oreo" because I "talk white," but when I enter a room, I am always foremost black.

Or rather, I am a black body. Depending on the space and audience, I may be black skin, brain, eyes, nose, mouth. Or I may be black skin, mouth, breasts, thighs, pussy, ass. I may be invisible. When do I get to be human?

FLESH

BLACK GIRL SABBATH

IT FEELS FRAUDULENT to be writing this on a day when I haven't washed my hair, but these days are frequent and many. By washing, of course, I mean the literal cleaning, I mean invoking the powers of shampoo and combing through the naps; I mean wash day. Alternatively: the black girl's sabbath. Because what else should happen on wash day besides the acts of washing and conditioning and a full day of relaxation? On occasion, I'll spend my wash days doing work. Depending on the mood of the day and how I woke up, I might grade all day, or I might binge-watch a television show I've already seen or a newly released season. Understand how much wash day means to me, because these uninterrupted days are rare, and I don't get much time to meditate and be with myself. When a black woman tells you it's wash day, the protocol for bothering her is don't, because this is the sabbath, and it's to be respected.

I have a complicated relationship with my hair. I love my hair, but I also know that my hair texture is a loose result of oppression and the remnant of a past that lingers below the surface. My mom says that "the white" comes out in my hair. Most likely, the European blood in my DNA tracks back to some ancestor on either side of my family (potentially both) and non-consensual sex—not necessarily rape—but sex with an unequal power dynamic. My great-grandmother on my father's side ran a brothel with her best friend, a white woman, whose father owned the place. My grandmother is the product of my great-grandmother and her best friend's father—a biracial woman who passed as white, and in the early 1900s if you could pass as white, then you were white. My curl pattern is different from my sister's, she's got that Angela Davis fro, which she can manipulate into various protective styles, and easily twist up at night. I can't even blow-dry a section of my hair straight without hurting my arms and getting stressed out. My natural hair also hides a past. It's not a secret, but if you didn't know me prior to 2009, then you can't even tell that for the majority of my life, I had dreadlocks. Thirteen years of dreadlocks, before they became all the rage and on-trend, back when people assumed dreadlocks meant you were a Rastafarian, a stoner, or both. But I was neither. My entire family had dreadlocks. It was a cost-effective lifestyle, that paid its price in being teased by everyone who had never seen someone with dreadlocks before. It's amazing how easily stereotypes can affect one's life, even as a child, even after you've grown and cut them off. I expected an afro to be easy. I didn't expect to have to do anything, I didn't know I had to do anything; I had not grown up doing anything to my hair besides washing it and braiding it. And then I cut it all off, terrified and thrilled by the consequences of having short hairs: the teeniest of afros, and how that would affect any semblance of beauty I might have had.

The first few years, I only picked out my hair a few times a week, hating the sound of my dry hair ripping apart. Once in the library, a black boy in the grade above me pulled out his metal pick—one of those with the black power fist on the handle—and, without my consent, began picking my hair out in the library. As I sat talking with friends, he stood behind me critiquing the nappiness of my hair and combed it out to its full volume, an imitation of his own afro. "You need this, just let me do this," he kept repeating. I rolled my eyes and acquiesced. Tenderheaded, I flinched each time his pick got caught on a knot of hair. My friends' eyes watched him behind me, combing and shaping, turning the library into a barbershop. When he was finished, feigning exhaustion, my afro was long and voluminous, a kinky halo around my face. For the first time, someone could have combed their fingers through my hair without them getting caught.

At first, I only used two hair products: shampoo and leave-in conditioner/hair lotion. I used the pink bottle of hair lotion that was greasy on the hands and hair, too liquid-y to be true, and my hair drank it up like water to a cactus. Sometimes, I used the green bottle of hair lotion: olive oil–based, thicker than the pink, but still greasy on the hands and hair, sticking to the hair on my head instead of nourishing it. And then there was my leave-in conditioner, the clear bottle with pink accents, the twin to my favorite shampoo, but sticky and greasy, leaving my hair parched and thirsting for moisture. The curls on my head would dry out so quickly, caked in conditioner, white and flaky.

It wasn't enough to own shampoo and conditioner. Black hair requires a process of trial and error. Hair constantly fluctuating as it grows, affected by diet and lifestyle, and the prod-

ucts I once used might not always do the trick. I like washing
my hair, or rather, I like getting my hair wet almost every time
I shower. I am not an exemplary black girl when it comes to
my hair. There are women who treat their hair like the crown it
is, tending to it often and prioritizing it above everything else.
They have all the products, they have the trusted hair stylist,
and most likely, they grew up doing these hair rituals, having been passed down the traditions of black hair care from
their own mothers, aunts, grandmothers, sisters, and cousins.
I didn't grow up with hair rituals, so I don't protect and maintain it as well as I could. I don't wrap my hair at night, I don't
sleep on a silk pillowcase, and I don't wear protective styles
in the winter (for now). I don't nap sitting up after getting my
hair done, so I get bed head. My afro crooked to one side and
flat in the back like I've had the best sleep of my life. But I
can't walk out of the house every day with a nappy fro, and
finger-combing can only bring so much dignity back to a day-
old, unkempt afro. I'd rather start over with freshly washed
hair. But the problem, or blessing, of black hair is that oil is
life. Oil is the blessing from the ancestors that keeps everything in check. It is essential. If I shampoo every day, I strip
my hair of the oils it needs to thrive, but if I just let water soak
in my highly porous hair all day, I'll smell because my hair
takes hours to (barely) dry. A dilemma. A conundrum.

Then I found co-wash. A very simple infographic on the
internet spelled it out for me. Two words: cleansing conditioner, it does everything shampoo does without stripping the
oils. I hunted around the small "multicultural" and "ethnic"
hair care sections for co-wash, my soon-to-be favorite product. But my co-wash was not in the ethnic hair care section.
Instead, it was with the rest of its brand family in the enor-

mous non-ethnic hair care section, a triad of brown bottles near the floor. One of those brown bottles said CO-WASH FOR NATURAL HAIR, so I grabbed it, already having trusted the brand with my hair before when it was just for curly-haired individuals, but my hair isn't just curly; it is kinky, untamed, and in control.

I began using co-wash in college, one weekend, initiating a new ritual. I liked to get high and wash my hair. Someone had told me that taking showers while stoned was incredible, so I tried it, of course. My rainbow rhinoceros pipe, Remy, was stowed underneath my sink between boxes of feminine pads, cleaning supplies, hair products, and toilet paper. I turned on the shower first—to get the hot water going full blast, near scalding—and sat on the toilet packing my bowl as the room filled with steam. I'd smoke half the bowl, set it on the sink, turn on an album to blast through my Bluetooth speaker, and step into the shower. Since I didn't have to pay a water bill for my apartment, a shower could last anywhere from ten to forty minutes. I'd start feeling stoned about fifteen minutes into my shower, right after I'd gotten through my initial think session and before I started washing my hair. With co-wash (and many other black hair care products) they say, "less is more," but I'd squeeze two palmfuls and apply it to my thick, sopping wet hair, massaging my fingers deep onto my scalp, trying to spread the co-wash everywhere, leaving no curl uncoated. Then it had to set. The bottle says three minutes, I always aimed for ten. I'd shave my legs. Wash the rest of my body. Pantomime concerts. Exfoliate my neck and face. Think more. Eventually, I'd grab my wide-tooth comb or afro pick and start combing through my curls, using my fingers to comb or rip apart the tough sections of nappy hair. Stoned, it didn't hurt as much as it typically did to pull a comb through my thick mess of curls—similar to the dense patch of thickets Simba chased Rafiki through in *The Lion King*. After a slightly painful combing, I'd be standing underneath the showerhead, deep massaging my scalp to rinse out the co-wash and any uprooted curls and understand why strangers and friends loved to coax their fingers into my afro without permission. My hair is soft and thick; the kind of hair that would be considered "good" by a woman who believes there's such a thing as "bad" hair.

In Chris Rock's 2006 documentary *Good Hair*, he attempts to answer the questions "what is good hair," and "where did that terminology come from?" After asking black women, black men, and Indian manufacturers of human hair, Chris Rock stands on the street with an afro and attempts to sell it. Later, he goes into stores, trying to sell his "black hair" and "African hair," but no one will buy it. It is not sexy enough. One shop owner implies that it's not "healthy" for him to sell it in his store. Another shop owner points out the fact that black women don't even wear their own natural hair. *Good Hair* is outdated, but what is said about "good" hair versus "bad" hair remains the same. "Good" hair leans toward standards of European beauty: straight, silky, long. Black hair doesn't do that naturally. By these definitions, my hair is not "good," and I don't want it to be. But if I were to straighten it, then its perceived quality would change. I hate straightening my hair—the entire three- to five-hour process is not worth the two weeks of long, silky hair I have to maintain. I feel ugly with straight hair, something about its limpness seems to not fit the frame of my face. I've had my hair straightened several times, each time as randomly as the one before. Once, I was able to slide into a spot at my mother's hairdresser when I went with her to get her hair done. The first time, my friends swarmed me at a sleepover and begged me to let them straighten it. Only once have I actually made an appointment. Other times, my cousins decided to accept the challenge whenever I came to visit, reminding me that I should get my hair straightened regularly for maintenance. In 2014, I decided to stop straightening my hair; each time, I'd felt like I'd lost my personality even as the women around me complimented its length, sheen, and straightness, even as I was able to whip my hair from side to side and brush it from my face. But straight hair, "good hair," just wasn't for me.

It didn't help that when my hair grew thicker and longer, I was faced with the complicated truth of curl patterns and hair type. My hair took more than a day to dry fully, it refused to cooperate with any styling, shrinking up as it dried throughout the day. Whenever my hair had fully dried, people who saw me regularly would ask if I'd gotten my hair cut. I was never sure how to explain shrinkage to non-black people. My hair looks shorter because it's no longer wet or stretched. It's very simple, but cultural differences are difficult to understand. If someone pointed out my shrinkage, I would take it as a note that I'd need to wash my hair again, rather than explaining that shrinkage is my everyday, my normal. My hair texture is made up of zig-zags, sharp bends, curls, and kinks, combining into a single tangled mess I battle every day. I'd tried everything: shampoo and conditioner, straightening, combing, co-washing, but nothing was working to keep my hair clean, untangled, and long at the same time. My college years, practically every moment photographed, provided a close look at my hair growth. I'd arrived at school in North Carolina with a tiny afro, barely maintained with a daily rinse and weekly shampoo, an afro pick and moisturizer. Over the years, my afro bloomed from kinky curls clinging to my scalp to loose black, dyed red, and bleached blonde curls framing my face and spiraling out in different directions.

Cosmopolitan published an article about how to have kinky hair . . . by using a crimping iron. This is one of the moments where white audiences and black vernacular don't mix. In the non-black world, kinky is a sexual behavior. One is kinky, one has kinks. Using blindfolds in the bedroom is a kink. And then there is my kinky hair. The *Oxford English Dictionary* has the earliest usage of the word "kinky" on January 6, 1844, in the *Congressional Globe*; it says: "[The Negro's] skull is as thick, his hair is as kinkey, his nose as flat . . . as the day he was first introduced." The next entry is also racist, taking place in 1848; the following, in 1861; and it continues from there. It is not used in a different way until 1889 as a colloquial for "queer, eccentric, crotchety," and then finally in 1959 as a term for unconventional sexual behavior. The primary *OED* definition:

adj, 1. Having, or full of, kinks; closely curled or twisted: said esp. of the hair of some races.

Black hair. Negro hair. According to the definition, it is impossible for a white person to have kinky hair, assuming that the *OED* is directed towards a primarily white audience. So, the *Cosmo* article is how to appropriate it: small, crimped curls, so they look tightly together. The models look like early 2000s Barbie dolls, the ones that came with long crimped blonde hair, a style my cousins loved to wear. Yes, my hair is kinky.

Yes, kinky is a term intended to other entire races from European ones (because why not use "curly" to describe tight curls?). A prime example of an oppressive rhetorical move to other a body and boost European and white supremacy.

It wasn't until I graduated from college that I had enough free time to experiment with my hair again. Once again, I went to the internet, scrolling through hundreds of black women offering tips and tutorials to maintaining and styling natural hair—a community I'd always been a part of, but was resurfacing and beginning to thrive again. These women were willing to be the guinea pigs for styling: They tried and reviewed products, made videos of their styling processes, and created infographics and tools for natural women like me who had no idea what worked and weren't willing to waste money on products that might not. On the internet, black women were promoting detangling hair with deep conditioner: a time-consuming process that would result in length and more options in styling. Even though I hated combing my hair, I went to the store to look for deep conditioner. I wanted long hair again, or at least hair that would resist shrinkage, that I could style and wear something other than bows and athletic headbands.

I chose a deep conditioner by a brand that my mom knew and trusted. The white tub consisted of a thick and heavy white gel, that I was supposed to apply to wet hair, comb through, and rinse. But the black women guiding me through my first detangling sessions via YouTube told me to let the deep conditioner set for at least thirty minutes for maximum penetration to the root. I applied globs of deep conditioner to my hair, trying to spread it as evenly as possible over every curl and surface of my head. I put a shower cap on afterwards because every woman said that heat helps the penetration. In one tutorial, a woman tied a plastic grocery bag as shower cap, which I later learned works just as well (and is cheaper). I let the deep conditioner set for two hours, which seemed appropriate for the length and thickness of my hair.

The feeling of clean, healthy hair in your hands is incomparable. When I took off the shower cap, I was able to run my fingers through my heavily coated curls. I was armed with two wide-tooth combs and my afro pick. In front of the mirror, I started picking through all my curls, mixing in finger-combing as necessary, and then combing through all my hair again with a wide-tooth comb when I'd finished. Uprooted curls flew everywhere, landing in the sink, on the counter, and the bathroom floor. Already, my reflection was proving that my hair had grown a lot since I'd done the big chop. My curls, an ashy blonde color (a result of bleaching and purple highlights less than a year before), were finally displaying their true length and texture. For the past year, my hair had been just long enough to pull into a small ponytail puff, but only after having straightened my hair to its full length. In that state, my hair was still stretched enough while wet to bear more length than my typical afro. Looking at my deep-conditioned and rinsed hair, I knew I could style it into something bigger: a pineapple updo to sit on top of my head. It was tricky at first: wet hair slipping from my fingers and falling from my hands before I could trap it all into a hair tie. It took me three hours to complete the entire process, from the beginning of deep conditioning to the styling. My arms ached. My scalp was tender. My hair was wet, but lengthy and styled. I ended up spending the rest of the day on the couch with my family.

The language around black hair is strange: maximum penetration, conditioning, coat, relax, and straighten—it is indeed the taming of a beast. Listening to others describe their hair rituals fascinates me, because non-black people never discuss having to dedicate an entire day to maintaining their hair. Even when dyeing her hair, my roommate used a box and sat on the couch for an hour—no shower cap—to let it set. Does it not say "maximum penetration" on the back of the hair dye box? When I get highlights, the appointment takes four hours: an hour of which is me sitting underneath a dryer or with a shower cap on while the color is bleached away. Before natural hair became popular again, having straight hair was the standard, be it the way of weave, wig, or chemical relaxer. Black women used to condition their curls to be straight, literally breaking the curl pattern with chemicals so it would become limp and obedient to the flat iron or hot comb. Now, deep conditioning is training curls to be fuller and looser, so we can stretch them out more by twisting, banding, and blowing out. Maybe this is why black women love to talk about hair so much? We wake up every day facing the struggle of what to do, how to style, how much time do I have, am I wetting my hair today, do I have a hat, is my hair twisted, will my twist out actually come out right? There are a lot of components in learning to do black hair and training that hair to cooperate. The language makes it seem impossible, but it's a matter of patience and experimenting.

I started having regular wash days when I went to graduate school. I only had class three days a week, so I'd wash my hair on Friday, Saturday, or Sunday, depending on if I had plans. Sundays were preferable though; it was rare to have plans on Sundays. I lived with a white woman, and I never explained the concept of wash days to her. I simply did them and hoped she didn't get in my way. I always woke up first: traipsing half-naked through the living room to the bathroom (next to her bedroom) to take a long, hot shower. Our bathroom was cramped: shower, bath, toilet, sink, radiator pipe, very small window, and no ventilation. The steam was stifling. Afterwards, I'd apply deep conditioner to my hair, put it in a ponytail and throw on a shower cap before leaving the bathroom. I set my timer for two hours, during which I'd make breakfast, watch Netflix while eating, and then do work: reading in my bed or writing. By the time my timer went off, my roommate would usually be eating breakfast in the living room while watching TV. I'd march past her into the bathroom with all the essentials: leave-in conditioner, hair towel, old t-shirt (for drying), three hair ties (two regular-sized, one overstretched), hair clips (for parting), wide-tooth comb, afro pick, and Bluetooth speaker for blasting albums to drown out the sound of my hair ripping. My roommate never asked, and I'm not sure she knew what I was doing in the bathroom for hours at a time after having already taken a shower. I'd come out with a fresh new hairdo or my hair wrapped in a dampened t-shirt and return to my room to watch television, do homework, read, write, or talk on the phone with my best friends.

These are my favorite days: wash days, the black girl sabbath. When I'm at home during the holidays, I spend wash day with my sister, helping her to set up the deep-conditioning process before binge-watching *Scandal* or *How to Get Away With Murder* on Netflix for hours. Her hair is shorter than mine, but easier to comb. When she went to college, she began wrapping her hair in silk scarves at night to keep it moisturized, having protective styles done, and using an African oil as her go-to product. Sometimes, we revert to the nostalgic way of black girls helping each other with their hair, and we'll rinse our hair out in the kitchen sink, running the faucet over the other's head while she stands with her neck craned into the sink, holding the corners of a towel over her eyes. These days, when I've finished deep conditioning and detangling, I'll put my hair into afro puffs, mini buns, or pineapple hairdos. My sister will twist her own hair or sit on the floor between our mom's legs to have her hair plaited. There are days that I leave my deep conditioner in overnight, combing it all out the night before and rinsing it the next morning. Other days, I will hide my shower cap–covered hair underneath a head scarf or beanie and go to work or run errands.

Wash day is sacred. It's one of the few days that a black woman can simply ignore the rest of the world and focus on herself and loved ones. On wash day, there is no white supremacy or patriarchy, no oppression-induced anxiety, no microaggressions, no mean mugs, no cat calls, nothing that makes us feel less. I do my best to ignore these things or bury away the more stressful duties of life as a black woman. This is my day off. I am too busy losing myself in books, self-care, art-making, cooking, and sometimes friendship. There should be candles and television and music. There should be food that makes the soul happy. There should be shea butter–scented prayers and wishes. There should be incense and flowers, water and wine. There should be coconut oil melting in the palm of her hands. I should feel the ancestors in the room— hair locked, body moisturized, scarves wrapped perfectly, skin healthy and glowing—blocking all the negative energy from reaching her. Tomorrow, those cultural biases and inequalities will return to stifle me (and my curls). But not on the sabbath.

ME, MY FAT, AND I

I

I used to tell people that if I just lost a hundred pounds then everything would be perfect. Because if I lost a hundred pounds, then maybe someone would be able to fully love me, instead of loving only parts of me, but never the whole. If I lost a hundred pounds, I wouldn't shrink away from the mirror when my friends and I are getting dressed to go out, and one of them complains about how fat they are, tugging at tight skin. If I lost a hundred pounds, I thought that maybe the self-love would just appear naturally, that maybe I'd wake up one morning and stare at myself without self-loathing in the bathroom mirror.

Once, I told my cousin that I needed to lose a hundred pounds. She said, "Don't be ridiculous, if you lost a hundred pounds you'd die."

As the biggest person in the room, I put myself down before anyone else can. Hoping that by calling myself fat, big, bigger, or biggest, no one else would need to point it out. But instead, I'd create a hush in the room, a swelling silence, until someone would finally say: "You're not fat." Maybe, but I'm also not stupid. I can look in a mirror and see for myself. But the "you're not fat" statement always made me wonder if I was delusional, if my brain was hard-wired to see more than what was really there.

So, I started grabbing my fat. I'd stand in the mirror before or after the shower, fully naked or half-naked, trying not to look myself in the eyes as I gauged the situation for myself. Both hands pulling and pushing the fat around my belly; both lungs, sucking in. Turn sideways: one hand lifts a butt cheek, pinches the inside of each thigh; the other arm outstretched, shaking to see the arm fat jiggle. Finally, one hand on each breast, lifting them up before turning to the side, and then to the front, letting go to see if they were symmetrical. A few bounces on the balls of my feet to see all of the excess moving at once. I stare at myself and imagine the surgical site markings, the dashes around my stomach, my inner thighs—there would be more ink on my body than skin.

One of the problems with being fat is having to decide what is skinny, finding someone to compare myself to. I wasn't comparing myself to Beyoncé or Rihanna—I was comparing myself to my friends as we stood side by side in photos, as we ate lunch together, as we changed in the locker room, as we lay by the pool, as we checked ourselves out in the mirror. My friends were skinny and most of them were white. They were also tall, healthy, filled out, proportionate. They didn't have belly fat or breast spillage or cellulite. Very few of my friends could be considered chubby or thick, but none of them ugly. And as puberty filled and stretched them out, I remained short, thickening in the middle: my thighs, my hips, my stomach, but these were not curves, this was simply fat, sitting on my muscles and bones not budging, just expanding.

II

It wouldn't be fair of me to discount the boys and men who wanted me. The ones who grabbed my ass, slid their hands down my shirt, and spread my thighs. I could never forget them if I wanted to, because they taught me that fat people are still desirable, and they made me feel like I was worth something, before proving that that I wasn't. The discrepancy between actions and words is crucial, though I ignored the inconsistencies. I relished their hot breath against my neck and hands on my waistline, even as they dated and lusted after other women. I ignored that sometimes they were only interested in my brain and other times my body, but never all of me at once. I ignored the feeling of emptiness inside me each time I gave a little bit of myself, after they'd left me in the dark, alone again with my thoughts. I began to believe that sadness and sex went together. I ignored the possibility that the word "love" could be a tool, like a screwdriver or pliers, used to simply open things.

I tested out my sexuality. Everything I did was calculated: the flirting, the touching, the permitting, the submitting. Was I attractive? Was I beautiful? Could I be sexy? Could I make a man want me? These are the questions I should have asked the boys and men, instead of spending my alone time rewinding our interactions for analysis. I wanted to know why. Why did they want me? Why were they so forward? What about me had changed?

To the boys and men who wanted me: You never called me beautiful, and you never asked me what I wanted before clambering on top of me and seeking out your own POV fantasy. To the boys and men who wanted me: I wouldn't have let you have me if I had known I was a fetish. Because why else did you want to fuck the fat, dark-skinned girl? Choose: fat or dark-skinned, which one got you off more? Once I considered that I was a fetish, I disassociated from my body. I couldn't trust anyone. Do you really like me? Or do you just want to fuck me and disappear? You can cross me off your bucket list now. You can tell your friends about me, draw them a map to opening my body. Isn't that why you came? You don't really know me. What's my favorite Michael Jackson song? How do you pronounce my name? What color are my eyes? Do you even care?

I didn't learn to hate myself. I think it's something that just happened to me, and I repeated it enough to myself that I began believing it. I'm not sure I had learned to love myself before I felt the disgust. It only takes a few people unwilling to love you before you believe you're unlovable. I was nothing more than a body to fall into, an urge to satisfy, a box to check. I was an on-demand service. I watched the boy I loved choose everyone but me, and when I asked him why, it was because I was not enough. I was not skinny enough. I was not curvy enough. I was not flexible enough. I was not reckless enough. I was not submissive enough. I was not happy enough. I did not love myself enough.

And I reminded myself that I was not enough every second of every day that he wasn't there to distract me. I reminded myself that I was not enough before another boy or man had the chance to remind me or say the opposite. I believed I was not enough until I was not enough for myself.

I didn't believe I could be more than a desire.

I never imagined that I could be enough, or maybe even too much for someone else to love. I never imagined that I was some*one*, instead of some*thing*, to be deserved.

Finally, I locked myself away, prematurely putting myself in the friend zone, diving deep into my education. I became afraid to look men in the eye because I could feel them undressing me or ignoring me, always one or the other. The men undressing me would squint their eyes and follow me in silence. Sometimes, they looked at me like a puzzle they couldn't solve. The men ignoring me had empty eyes and breezed past me, looking beyond me. On the street, I put my head down or pulled out my phone; I'd ignore them first. Involuntary celibacy evolved into a preference. Men became objects to me—look, but don't touch. As I took my romantic and sexual hiatuses, I tried to fall in love with myself. So, when an acquaintance told me he could release my stress through sex, I laughed at him. Later, when I was stoned and doing dishes, he cornered me in the kitchen and whispered, "I never been with a big girl before." I laughed again. I laughed at the come-on, I laughed at the fetish, and I laughed because, once again, I was just another item on another man's list.

I walked away from him still laughing, "You couldn't handle me."

III

I tried losing weight. I went to the gym. I had a personal trainer. I started drinking water more. I snacked on fruit and vegetables. But eventually, I had to come to terms. I needed to learn how to love my body as is.

It seems like everything and everyone in the world was telling me that in order to have everything I wanted, I needed to be skinny. And then, society began turning against promoting thin bodies and flawless features, pushing imperfections to the forefront of sexy: stretchmarks and thick thighs, a roll here or there. The notion was that women who had a little extra mass, maybe (using doctor verbiage) overweight but not obese, could be considered "thick," but women who had a lot of extra mass? Those of us fortunate enough to know our BMI—not because we cared, but because a doctor showed us a chart to explain that we were morbidly obese—we were only attractive to the men who wanted to smother their faces in our breasts and curl up with us at night. Obese thick was more of a fetish than an attraction. It was debatable if women with several fat rolls and thighs dimpled with cellulite could be considered thick too. Some women who became the bodies and faces of "thick" didn't want to include other big women. For them, thick was strictly for the pear-shaped and hourglass-framed, the three-to-four-stretch-marks-only women. A surge of women on Instagram without any fat rolls began claiming "thick" and "fat," constantly posting videos and pictures of their half-naked bodies for their audiences.

But men began throwing the word "thick" around like women were nothing more than a slice of bacon, pinning it onto whichever woman they deemed good enough, whose body met a skewed criteria. I didn't want to be "thick" or slipped into a loose category of women fitting men's standards and obsessions. I don't think I was confident enough to be thick, to flaunt my body publicly with all its imperfections. Maybe being "thick" to women is more of a mentality than a body image, maybe it means "I am comfortable with my body, it does not define me." And then there is me: uncomfortable in my body, fat, not thick.

Of course, there are the people who truly love bigger women, and I am forced to step back and wonder: Is this a fetish or natural attraction? Does this man want me because I fit his type or because he is attracted to everything about me, inside and out?

I didn't meet other fat women until college. My college was predominantly white, and most of the white women looked the same: straight hair, leggy, small-chested. The black women were all incredibly different, so we cliqued up based on interests and living arrangements instead of looks. My friends were still skinny, but I was meeting women who wore something above a size 8. These women didn't hate themselves. They dressed well and navigated campus exuding the confidence I thought I had in high school—before the boys, before the fetish—and I wanted that again. I gained fifty pounds my freshman year: I was extremely depressed, I didn't work out or play a sport, I consumed a ridiculous amount of Cookout Cajun fries and milkshakes. My sophomore year, I was still depressed and trying to squeeze my changing body into the same clothes that I had worn before I gained weight. I didn't know where plus-size women shopped. I didn't know if I could even consider myself plus-size since I was short and shapeless. I did not have curves that dresses could hug; my shape was cylindrical: up, down, and wide.

Jeans were the last straw. I'd been buying jeans from Target and was constantly having to replace them after the friction between my thighs quickly ruined them. I needed to find jeans that wouldn't shred. I randomly stumbled upon Torrid through an internet ad on Hot Topic. It seemed hidden away from the world, but is a paradise for anyone larger than a size 12, full of cute, youthful clothes. I bought a test pair of jeans: a pair of light-wash denim with a white floral print. They fit like a glove, accentuating my hips as if I had a curve and lengthening my body as if I were over five-foot-three. I never wanted to take them off. I bought another pair in dark wash. For the first time in a long time, someone took a photo of me where I exuded confidence in a glow. And for the first time in a long time, I looked at a photo of myself smiling without feeling that the smile was lie.

IV

When I first sat down to write this, I wrote the first sentence and cried. I was confused about why I was crying, though I knew why. But still, how could I have hated myself that much? People who had no business telling me how to live my life were asking me why I hadn't gotten a breast reduction, would I get gastric bypass surgery, when would I switch to the liquid detox or protein-rich diet? I spent years trying to be like the people who surrounded me: hourglass figures, subtle abdominal muscles, two-piece bathing suits, crop tops, and plunge tops. I spent years trying to feel less like an object and more like a person.

We all have body image issues: We want what the other has. The skinny girl wants the fat girl's double-Ds and the white girl wants the black girl's butt; the fat girl wants the skinny girl's collarbone and the black girl just wants the white girl's respect. We're looking for external validation from our partners, our bosses, our families and when we don't get it, the chest of self-loathing looming inside us creaks open a little more.

It's taken me a long time to learn how to love myself for myself. And a combination of celibacy, ambition, and a style upgrade. My closet transformed from a teenager's filled with sweatpants, sneakers, and graphic t-shirts, to a young adult's, with blazers, slim-cut jeans, and heels. I bought bras that actually held a form, jeans that didn't sag in the back or shred between the thighs, simple t-shirts and tank tops; midi-skirts and trousers. I stopped considering how a man would react to what I wore or how I presented myself. I concerned myself instead with making sure I wasn't overly dressed for the occasion. There was no romance. There were men—acquaintances, friends, strangers, and some of them tempted me to dive back into the lifestyle of being an object of pleasure—but I waved them off as distractions. I focused on honing my talents: making art more, writing more, researching more, presenting more, reading more. I focused on learning how to love myself and enjoy being alone. I took myself on "dates," eating out at restaurants alone, going to see movies alone—during my first week in Chicago, I walked from the Magnificent Mile to Navy Pier, sweating through my t-shirt and continuing to walk until I reached the end of the pier, and sat on a bench to watch the water by myself. I didn't want to attach myself to anything or anyone having moved to a new place, so I looked for and tried to understand myself better.

People noticed. My friends and family began complimenting me on my clothes, health, and skin. Though the self-loathing—born out of not being loved back, but still giving everything I had to a boy who would never love me back—is still there, buried deep, it has receded. I've gained real confidence, the kind that reveals itself in my work, appearance, and presence. My skin is clear and clean. My hair is long and healthy. And I'm still fat. My weight annoyingly fluctuating up and down, regardless of changes to my diet and exercise. I still don't think I'm beautiful. If you think so, please don't tell me.

I won't believe you if you tell me that I'm beautiful. I'm not there yet. But I will take the compliment and pocket it for later. Right now, I give myself a nod of approval when I'm getting dressed in the morning; when I'm standing in front of the mirror with toothpaste on my face and a bath sheet wrapped around my body; when I'm sweating because I've walked halfway across the city in a skirt. I'm looking at the natural glow, the hint of happiness in the apple of my cheeks, the visible comfort in my skin. That's where I see beauty. I will see the same beauty when I dare to not wear a tank top underneath that sheer top, when I choose flats over heels on a night out, or when I wear my pants high-waisted with a tucked shirt. I'm over trying to lose weight and contort myself in order to get somewhere in life, to be desirable, to feel pretty—I'm better than that. My work speaks for itself and it does not submit to the pinching and extracting by people who want me to contort to their own aesthetic. I am my own aesthetic. So, I will decorate my body with however many tattoos I want and wherever I please, no matter if there's a roll, a crease, or a few stretch marks crawling their way to the area. I will wax and shave, or sometimes I won't. I will sleep naked and let gravity have its way with my body. I'm working on myself by myself, but one day I will believe in the same beauty you claim to see today. Just give me time.

THUNDER THIGHS

I **CARVED MYSELF A VENUS** in ceramics once, using the pads of my thumbs and fingernails to sculpt her out of red clay. She had hips where I have none and her breasts were perkier than mine, firmer, but I made her body thick like mine and I gave her thunder thighs. Around her legs, a snake coiled tightly, its body climbing up her thighs with large gaps between the coils because she was a woman: Venus and Eve, wrapped in one, wrapped in sin. My Venus: headless, midriff peeking, with thunder thighs.

I don't have a thigh gap and looking in these magazines and at these online models, I'm wondering if I should be trying to have a gap between my thighs—a gap for whom? A gap for me? A gap for you? A gap for anyone to imagine sliding into me with ease and attempting to clutch for my spirit, mistaking love for pleasure, pain as pleasure. I don't have a thigh gap. When I wear shorts and skirts, my thighs are constantly touching, constantly creating friction: fabric on fabric, fabric on skin, skin on skin. When I draw women, I draw a line between their legs: a simple line, curved.

She asks if I am looking at her blackened thighs (I'm not) before going on a tangent about how she read once that men think of the darkened insides of women's thighs to hold off on coming, to counter their pleasure, to prolong release. The inside of my thighs transition in color from my normal brown skin tone to a blackened brown, rippled with cellulite. I try to imagine a lover trying to make himself last by looking at my thighs, the same ones that didn't stop him from entering me in the first place. He can't stop, and he doesn't stop, allows himself to take the cold gulp of orgasm—soft like putty between black thighs.

Sometimes, I grab the fat of my thighs and wonder why I didn't get liposuction when I had the chance. I worked at a plastic surgery center, I knew that liposuction and Cool Sculpting worked. I'd organized the before and after photos. Of course, I never really had the chance—I couldn't afford it. Sometimes, I wonder why I didn't keep exercising and playing sports, even though I had to keep throwing away sweatpants, the fabric pilling away inside the thighs from years of daily use. Sometimes, I think everything I eat only goes to my thighs, like that episode of *Spongebob Squarepants* when Squidward binge-eats all those Krabby Patties, thighs rippling with cellulite, a colossal pedestal for his slim upper body. He explodes.

I got a thigh tattoo because I hated my thighs, because I wanted to be reminded of my own strength because I wanted to put more art on my skin. At the consult, I pull up my shorts and tell the tattoo artist that she has a large canvas and I'd like this bear with the pose of this other bear and a constellation here and watercolor and can she do it. Bears mean a lot to me because of their strength, solitude, maternity, and curiosity. They are powerful animals.

A few months later, on a trip back home, I pull off my sweatpants in the tattoo parlor and let her draw on me with needles. My thighs pool in sweat as my left leg muscle spasms uncontrollably—my right one still. She won't let me look. I bite back on the pain, try to flex my left leg without shifting; I want to sleep. The bear is beautiful: With textured fur, it is mid-walk towards my inner thigh, standing over the Ursa Major constellation and a swirl of blue, purple, and green watercolors. The entire tattoo is galactic, floating on my mass of thigh, seeping deep into the layers of my skin. The tattoo artist wipes the dotting blood off my thigh before taking a photo for Instagram. She coolly wraps my thigh in saran wrap, which begins to awkwardly bunch up and fall as soon as I put my sweatpants back on. This thigh is beautiful, this thigh is edgy, this thigh is art, this thigh has meaning. I begin to show off my thighs more: shorter dresses, short shorts. I want people to see me.

Fetty Wap raps "slim thick wit' yo cute ass, ayy" once, and all of the sudden everyone wants an hourglass woman to flip and fondle. So where do I fit in this world where they'll only want me if I'm both slim *and* thick. Slim thick is a meme. Slim thick is a lifestyle. But I am not at all slim thick with my black and educated ass, with my womanist self, with my thunder thighs, my natural hair, my cocoa skin, with my essaying self, my ink-riddled hands, with my attractive ass, my who cares about societal standards ass, my always on my grind ass.

Peel back the skin and see that my thighs are fat and muscle attached to femur, stretching from pelvis. My thighs that have been slapped, pinched, pulled, spread, caressed, bruised, cut, shaved, tattooed, held, hugged, rested on, sat on, gripped, and hated. How do I reclaim the forgotten parts of my body? Always hidden and yet, I am hyperaware of their existence, their friction. Is the answer in revealing them? Should I sit on the beach half-naked, thighs soaking in the sun? Should I stand nude in my windows, surveying the street? Is it a matter of photography or another tattoo? How do I make my body mine?

MESSY

BRIEF NOTES ON BODY POSITIVITY

WRITING ABOUT MY BODY IS DIFFICULT. I don't do my body enough justice by spilling my insecurities all over the page; but also, maybe I do her too much justice by ignoring her existence and giving her space to breathe. I am always trying to be objective. Even right now, I'd rather be doing anything else than discussing my body with you, than using my body to convince you that body positivity is everything.

When I think of body positivity, I think of Instagram: people who are considered plus-size radiating confidence through portrait photography, garnering thousands of likes with each post. That's great, but I can't do that—I won't do that. Instagram is shady. I've scoured the comments of plus-size women's posts and come across the trolls commenting about how disgusting and unhealthy their bodies are, as well as the men fetishizing them for their size. So, I wonder how body positivity exists outside of Instagram and for people like me, who know all their Instagram followers and interact with a small percentage of them.

I believe, more than anything, that body positivity is about truth. And it's hard for fat women and fat bodies to embrace and publicize that truth because it's hard for society to believe it. If enough people disregard your truth, you start believing the lie. The lie is that I'm unhappy, unhealthy, lazy, hypersexual, and desperate. The truth: I'm fat. Overweight. Obese. Too short to be this big. Too smart to be so confident about being this big. Too much. But I've always been the fat girl. From my knee getting stuck in the grate of my crib to eating popcorn naked in bed last night. There's nothing new about it. The only thing that's changed is that here I am, calling myself the fat girl, hoping my non-fat friends don't start doing the same (seriously, don't do it, don't call me fat).

Once, another fat girl called me fat in a public space, and I tried to chuckle away the fact that every single person in the room had begun staring at my jumpsuit, the one I'd thought was really cute until she said, "It's so hard to find cute fat clothes." The word "fat" aloud makes me cringe, puts me on the defensive. I have not reclaimed that word fully for it to escape from my mouth with confidence. Instead, it is awkward, trying to be cooler than it truly is, trying to belong to me. FAT. There are other words, I prefer none of them. THICK. BIG. BIGGER. OBESE. OVERWEIGHT. BBW. HEAVYSET. BIG GIRL.

In these moments, I lose my name. I am only a body. Bodies, like objects, are meant to be enjoyed, if not by its tenant then an intruder. Some bodies exist to be plundered. There is my body—

I'm not sure how she exists for others

—plundered, chased, exoticized, ignored, seen, objectified, loved, questioned, judged, disliked, dismantled, exposed, and forgiven, even when I have not apologized.

On the outside, I am unbothered and confident; but on the inside I consider every possible thought that goes through someone else's mind. Already, as a black woman, I police myself in many ways: I avoid anger in public, I nod and smile when my name is pronounced incorrectly; I allow men to be wrong; I bite my tongue and act weaker or dumber than I am to boost supervisors and men around me. So, I try to police my body to make other people comfortable. I tug at my clothing, shifting it into place to appear taller, thinner; to hide my body. I wonder if my face is too fat for my makeup. I watch myself in the mirror while working out, so I can glance around and see who else is watching my body tremble with each exercise. I dance near the safety of my table and friends. I buy clothes that are too big. I am more concerned about how comfortable other people are around my body than I am with how comfortable I am in my body.

Many times, my own friends have been openly fatphobic in front of me and I shrink away from the discussion, wondering if they think the same things about me when I'm not around, or I find myself defending strangers in public as an act of solidarity. And I hope that they'll read into my shock: *If you are so disgusted by their fatness, how do you feel about me?*

When people want to hurt me, it is always that I am fat, first. It stings a little, but often I wonder if people who attack my size don't consider that I've been swallowing fat jokes and insults my entire life. Like, you think I don't know that I'm fat? You think that I don't have a destructive relationship with food, bordering on obsessive, as I read the nutritional information on everything, give up sugar, eat sugar again, eat more protein, eat less altogether, drink more caffeine, drink only water—you think I haven't imagined slicing my body up to look how you want me to? And still, you remind me that I'm fat. You glance at my body, pay close attention to my clothing, watch me eat and drink. But I exist and I refuse to be forced into hiding or shame because other people don't like the way I look.

On New Year's Eve, I spent the whole night wondering if I should post a drunken bathroom selfie I took, where my crop top exposed my stretch-marked gut. Drunk me thought she looked fly as hell. In a crop top. With my belly out. There was a raw and unapologetic vibe to the picture, appropriate for New Year's Eve. I'd snuck away from my friends and the music to pee, and after enough tequila and lemonade, my friend's bathroom mirror was the perfect frame to a fat girl feeling herself a couple hours before midnight. I took seven sultry photos before someone eventually barged in to pee. It took me so long to decide to post it because I was concerned with what anyone would say, if they felt so pressed to comment. Who would make me regret posting this gratuitous picture of myself? But I looked fly as fuck, so I posted it. New year, bellies out. At 12:28 a.m. on January 1st, from the comfort of my bed, I finally posted the selfie with a caption that said: "A mirror pic where I was like okay belly we still cute *looking eyes/ black girl shrug*." I'm no Instagram influencer, but 64 people saw it. Only one person commented: "Incredible outfit."

Up to a point, I avoided mirrors and scales. Later, I stood in the mirror for too long, until my body warped into a mass of flaws. I forced my literal body into my work: writing, painting, creating, destroying. I have painted myself onto walls. I have photographed myself half-naked. I have morphed myself into feature-less silhouettes; become a vector file, an InDesign draft; a laser-cut acrylic plate. I have viewed my body so objectively and criticized myself as an object separate from myself, that it makes sense I would begin to find my flaws interesting. The way my right shoulder is angled, while the other is not. The gap in my teeth. The moles and beauty marks. The uneven number of rolls. Have my thighs ever not touched? My small, but wide, feet. The ligament that snaps back and forth over my kneecap with a popping sign. My fucked up knees. My straight hips that led to the fucked up knees. My flat butt. (I see those squats working though!) The constant frown: the way the corners of my lips point downward, always judging, always disappointed.

I'm not sorry if my body makes you uncomfortable. I spent enough time hating myself for being fat, I eventually forced myself to love it.

My body positivity comes in the forms of selfies and art, fashion and makeup, workout classes and dance floors, swimming and teaching. I enjoy all these things in my fat, black body, and have become less concerned with what others think as I do them. For me, "body positivity" is about being my truest self and surrounding myself with people who do the same. My best friends and I don't all look alike or fit into that clique-y version of friendship. Some of my favorite people are like me: tough exterior and marshmallow insides. But the others expose that vulnerability to the world, which is just as brave. And together we navigate the world awkwardly, confidently, experiencing the entire spectrum of emotions. We create spaces for ourselves instead of shrinking to fit into the spaces and roles others expect of us.

I've curated my Instagram and Twitter feeds to include models and influencers who are plus-size and share similar interests in makeup and fashion. I follow plus-size clothing brands, along with some of their models and brand ambassadors. I follow the #goldenconfidence hashtag to see a more diverse (and accurate) representation of fat people navigating the world around. I follow sex-positive people; I follow Planned Parenthood. Visual artists, makeup artists, tattoo hashtags and tattoo artists. I follow writers and bakers and foodies—and I believe that all these people (internet strangers and real-life friends) are body positive in their own ways. They are promoting their truths: This is my body, and this is how I enjoy it. They eat expensive food. They pay homage to their favorite childhood TV show by customizing a tattoo sleeve. They get annoyed with their pets. They brag about their children. They paint and collage. They grieve. They celebrate. They play LIFE. They sweat. They make mistakes. They cry a little when they laugh. I appreciate the normalcy, the highs and lows, because the truth is messy, raw, ugly, and disordered, which makes it beautiful and authentic.

So how do I remain body positive in the real world, without a hashtag, where every day I encounter people uncomfortable with my presence?

Take a dozen selfies. Wear a crop top in public. Paint my body on the walls of a gallery space and force people to look. Wear a thong, maybe not. Eat more than 20g of sugar in a day. Drop off homemade sugar cookies for my trainer. Skip the gym. Put myself first. Buy a two-piece bathing suit. Watch *KUWTK* on the treadmill. Eat while watching *My 600-lb Life*. Eat while watching *Hoarders*. Binge-watch TLC, Bravo, and BBC. Make a recipe from the no-sugar cookbook. Improve a recipe from

Pinterest. Run out of air from laughing too hard. Do a clay mask. Black tea with two Splendas. Tequila on the rocks with a lime. Put myself first. Dance with my eyes closed. Wear faux fur—flex in faux fur. Practice twerking in the kitchen and send the video to my best friend. See if people shirk at the word "fat." Scream. Paint my body and post it on Instagram. Take a selfie in my towel. Save nudes for later. Delete my Tinder. Remember that someone loved me once before, and someone will again. Put myself first. Eat a weed cupcake. Mix the José with Patrón. Sugar on the rim. Forget him when I'm on top. Put myself first. Red lipstick. No, black. Highlighter everywhere. Put myself first. Read my horoscope. Sing—loudly. Put myself first. Inhale through the nose. Put myself first. Exhale through the mouth. Put myself first. Put myself first. Put myself first.

THE ONE WHERE MY FEMME SWALLOWS YOU WHOLE

WE BOTH KNOW the water has never been your friend, and so the flood was always predestined to be your nemesis. And we both know that you could never know when I would finally come—when the 20 percent chance of rain would turn out to be a flash flood, when the tropical storm stewing on the coast for days would morph into a Category 3 or 5—and you can't stop me from my destination. Don't take it personally. Eighty-seven percent of everything on my way to you will be destroyed along with you: The trees will be ripped from the ground and tossed like lint from my shoulder, roof tiles will scatter in the wind, animals will flee or be swept with the current, and oh, the water— how it will rise like nothing ever seen before and at first, you will think it's God, but that is not my name. I fill your mouth by slinking through the gaps of your teeth, lubricating your throat as I trespass into your trachea with brute force, making my way into your lungs. Consumption is my obsession. You become what you desire, so the only thing I know to do is devour. I will be quick, I promise. The only trace of me will be inside you, claiming your body and spirit as mine. Afterwards, people will silently trek through the waterlogged ground in awe of what was strong enough to remain standing and everything else that was decimated in my path.

THE ONE WHERE MY FEMME HAS A PUNCH

AT FIRST it comes as a surprise that I am not as sweet and juicy as that other femme you tasted a while back, but there is something about me that makes your face twist up with displeasure and curiosity, and you want to relish in that paradox forever. What's the word? I'm bittersweet. An elixir of pessimism, creativity, laughter, rage, trauma, power, fear, and the liquidized form of sunshine, which could be water, or it might be honey, it all depends on the time of day and how the light reflects off me. All of that blended into a fierce body of acquired taste, a contemporary version of a body carved into the walls of caves and excavated from buried kingdoms—a body no one really wants anymore. I've got it. Plunge your teeth into my skin and there it is again: the punch—sour and intense, flooding your taste buds and slightly eroding your enamel, so your face pinches up because my flavor is unexpected but dependable, disappearing from your tongue and memory with a faint trace of something you want to have again. The feeling won't last forever, and maybe that's exactly how you like me: an explosion of bold flavor and light, a feeling you could never pin down—a supernova.

THE ONE WHERE
MY FEMME LOOKS
IN THE MIRROR

THIS IS AN ORIGIN STORY of how my femme came
to be. Or rather, how I came to understand myself
and my womanhood, how I learned to adapt and
evolve in different spaces. In so many ways, I am my truest
self on the page, where I interrogate everything about myself
and the world around me: my blackness, my sexuality, my gender, my worth, my femme.

•

I didn't start using the word "femme" to describe myself until
years of people labeling me as a femme woman. I didn't label
myself femme before then because I understood it to be a
term rooted in queer culture, and while I am an ally, many
people wouldn't consider me queer. I also worried that being
labeled as femme stripped me of one of my other identities or
twisted them all together in a way I couldn't imagine. Being
designated femme by my queer friends, seemed very similar
to being called an "honorary [insert identity]" with any other
word.

That is, until I took a writing workshop, specifically for women and femmes, where I was asked to define and deconstruct my femme, not my femininity. With each writing exercise, I tried to pinpoint exactly how I became aware of femininity, how I adopted and/or created that aesthetic, what it looked like, what it felt like, cementing that I didn't understand the differences between my femme and my femininity. In my mind, I presented a non-conformist femininity, rooted in a rejection of many feminine things I'd seen around me growing up.

And I knew that my femininity was complicated and had a lot to do with other aspects of myself: my blackness, my body, the spaces around me, language, and my sexuality. While other people in the workshop could express their femme selves beautifully on the page, I struggled to write something coherent, producing disjunctive work that didn't know what it wanted.

My breakthrough arrived later, in a craft seminar defining femme on our own terms, in our own terms. Our instructor defined femme as a term that is constantly evolving but tends to be used as a marker to help people connect with other aspects of their identity. We were asked, in what ways does your femme identity relate to your other identities? How does your femme identity define other aspects of your identity?

What would our femme look like in nature? if our femme was one of the five senses, which would it be? What has tried to destroy our femme and what has our femme given us? These were questions I could answer.

6/3—FEMME: A DECONSTRUCTION & RECONSTRUCTION

1) IN NATURE

BLACK BEAR—MATERNAL, SOLITARY, FIERCE,
BLACK, BRAVE, SMALL, CLIMB
LION—MATRIARCH, QUICK, STEALTH/OBSER-
VANT, LEADER, SOCIAL, HUNT, ROAR
SOLAR ECLIPSE—BLINDING / A SPECTACLE
LIGHTNING—BRIGHT, POWERFUL, DRAMATIC, QUIET
FLOOD—DESTRUCTIVE, TUMULTUOUS, UNCERTAIN, QUICK,
LASTING IMPACT
KOMODO DRAGON—FIGHTER, ~~POISONOUS~~ VENOMOUS, LAZY, THICK,
CARNIVORE/FOODIE, KING

2) THE SENSES

BITTERSWEET/SOUR—LIMES OR A MANGO THAT'S ALMOST RIPE;
SOUR GUMMY WORMS; SALTED CARAMEL
SIGHT: HEAVY CONTRAST / BOLD COLORS—TOO BRIGHT
SOUND: MIX CD WITH SOUNDTRACK, POP, HIP-HOP/R&B, ALTERNATIVE;
AN ERA; CRESCENDO
TOUCH: LINEN, HARDWOOD FLOORS; STAINLESS STEEL KNIVES; SILICONE

I came to realize that academia had tried to destroy my femme identity. As an educator, I have been boxed in and treated unfairly because of my sex, gender, age, and race. Each time I enter a classroom or a meeting, often as the only black body in the room, I am expected to surpass the talents and expectations of my white counterparts. I am expected to embody and possess the privilege that makes white men my superior. And so, I realized, men and religion also joined the ranks of top destructions to my femme identity, along with white feminism—pushing me to be many things I'm not: soft, submissive, silent, and sweet.

~~FAT~~ BLACK FEMME AS A LINEN LIGHTNING BOLT CRESCENDO

AND IN THE CLASSROOM, SHE COULD BE SO MANY THINGS, BUT FIRST AND FOREMOST SHE IS BLACK, THEN FAT, THEN TOO YOUNG TO BE A TEACHER. THE HARDEST PART IS KNOWING SHE HAS TO WEAR A DRESS AND BLAZER AND HEELS, WHEN SHE WOULD RATHER BE IN LEGGINGS AND A SWEATER, WOULD RATHER BE HERSELF, BUT THE RESPECT NEVER COMES WITH THE TERRITORY. AT FIRST, SHE IS SOFT WITH STUDENTS: MALLEABLE, COMFORTING—SHE ONLY WANTS THEM TO DO WELL. THE FIRST FEW WEEKS ARE THE HONEYMOON, AND THEY IGNORE THE CLAP OF THUNDER THAT SIGNALS THE STORM. FAT BLACK FEMME TRANSFORMS FROM SOFT-TO-TOUCH TO ELECTRIC, DEMANDING THE SAME RESPECT AS HER PEERS. BLAZERS TURN TO SWEATERS AND HEELS TURN TO UGG BOOTS LIKE SHE HAS TENURE. IN THE CLASSROOM, SHE BECOMES A SPECTACLE, THE ALL-KNOWING, AND STUDENTS LEARN THEY MUST RISE WITH THE STORM OR BE SWEPT AWAY, LOST TO THE CURRENT, FADED OUT OF SIGHT.

Most of the time, I am dressing for each day and occasion considering my comfort and unique style above everything else.

I am not trapped into a feminine presentation, but there are stereotypically feminine things that I enjoy wearing: lipstick, nail polish (really, to make sure I don't bite them all off), and earrings. And having a fat body with femme characteristics means that I will always be labeled femme or feminine regardless of what I wear because curves, long hair, and thick lips scream that I am biologically woman.

SHE CAN'T MAKE IT TOO EASY, OR SHE BECOMES A JOKE. SHE CAN'T BE TOO TOUGH, OR SHE IS OVERCOMPENSATING FOR HER BLACKNESS IN WHITE SPACES. SHE CREATES THE PERFECT STORM, A CRESCENDO OF RACE AND POP CULTURE AND LITERATURE TO DISRUPT FRAGILE BUBBLES AND EMPOWER THE STUDENT WHO FEELS UNSEEN. LIGHTNING CHAMPIONS THE DIFFERENT. AND SHE IS DIFFERENT—THE ONLY ONE LIKE HER. SHE IS THERE TO DISRUPT THE SLUMBERING SYSTEM OF ACADEMIA—A BRIGHT FLASH THEY NEVER SEE COMING.

When I consider things I do that are inherently femme, they all revolve around empowerment. How I feel when I walk into a room, how I command a space, how I interact with others—these are situations in which my femme roars to life and exists alongside and intertwined with the rest of my identities. My femme identity rejects a European patriarchal ideology, blooming from my existence as a black woman in a predominantly white space. I will not have my personhood judged by or compared to my white counterparts, man or woman.

Part of my femme is rooted in the understanding that I have always had to play both parts for myself: loved and lover. If I didn't love this fat, black body, no one else would. Of course, my femme didn't have a name here.

Many definitions of femme I've seen suggest that a femme identity requires two things: (1) one must present as feminine and (2) one must exist somewhere on the LGBTQ+ spectrum. As a demisexual woman who's attracted to men, I technically meet these requirements. But after I learned that demisexuality is a subsect of asexuality, and as my identity became more and more politicized in my work and existence, I came to believe that maybe "femme" was the word to describe how I navigated the world as a woman.

My body is disobedient. As in, my body and identities have always broken the rules, no matter how hard I have tried to abide them. So, I find myself asking, who has authority when it comes to marginalized people and their existence? The only authority I listen to is my mother—and even then, I only listen to what's practical. When it comes to this "traditional" authority, how has it become so entrenched in our world that we've spent decades having to renounce, destroy, and reject it in order to stake out equal space for ourselves?

So, I understand why it might ruffle feathers to call myself femme. But I also understand that I'm being judged on using a word that originally meant something specific and disobedient when first conceived in the American lexis. But now, forty-plus years later, that same word has evolved beyond its original aesthetic and into something more political, more unruly, used by queer and non-queer people to encompass a power and validate an existence. I'm not using femme like an abstract lamp you can buy at Urban Outfitters. My femme isn't pink and powdery, landing gracefully on your cheek. My femme has nothing to do with redefining femininity. My femme is political; she is living, breathing, and evolving with me, working alongside me to carve out this space—which feels like I have been carving endlessly—where I can exist. Who has the authority to strip away a form of my power without my permission? Who gave them the authority to put their hands on me?

THE ONE WHERE MY FEMME BRINGS YOU BACK TO LIFE

YOU FORGOT TO MARK ME on your calendar again, to pencil me in as a reminder that I would disappear for a couple minutes today and leave you in the dark. If you're not ready, that shit is frightening. Staring up into an abyss and wondering if the moon will return to its rightful place or if this is forever now—and absence of light and color. You hold your breath and wait. I'm curious to know what happens to you during the silence, the blackout, the solar eclipse as they call me. Early civilizations used to think it was the end of the world, they used to sacrifice their young to me, have wars because of me, drop to their knees and pray to me. You just don't do it like they used to. Now, you all sit there, staring through those clunky sunglasses, waiting for the day to return. What if I decided to leave you there, alone in the night? Your whole race would die out from the cold. Can you imagine the chaos? Maybe that's why I'm hiding out again: to deliver a tease of chaos. I'll be back though; you know I can't stand being in someone else's shadow. I just want to beat my personal record, take a few minutes for myself and make you sweat.

THE ONE WHERE MY FEMME SWELLS

T'S WRITTEN that I am supposed to make a dramatic entrance. This is the climax of the third act. After this, I won't return to the stage until the very end of the show. I absolutely have to give it my all. But I'm not worried, we've rehearsed this countless times—me and the band. We could do this with our eyes closed. It's become our love language. The strings tease me out as their fingers work their way up the scales and the hairs on their bow kiss them tenderly. The wind players have choreographed their breath to be simultaneous, a form of music in itself, as they control the air in their lungs to unwind the valve for me, slowly and intentionally. Here I come to enchant your ears with a velvet melody and hum, erupting with the rattle of drumsticks on snares—

You gasp, you weep, you applaud, and the curtain falls as I linger in the echo.

INTERLUDE

THE PART THUGS SKIP

T**ELL ME THE TALE** of how you met your lover, and I'll trade you mine. I hate to admit it, but I'm a sucker for the romantic. It is everything I've ever wished for and never had. Perhaps, it's better to say, I covet the romantic: the cuddling, flowers, doting, kissing, crying; all that shit. I'll tell you all about how sadness transformed into lust and into love for a spell before being repackaged into something empty and painful, silent and demanding. Tell me yours, I'll tell you mine. But pinky promise not to cry. This is one of those forbidden tales that breaks all the rules of attraction, one that bleeds into the true definition of romance—tragic and hilarious, comedic and sad. I'll spoil it for you: This love story doesn't have a happy ending. The ending is interpretive. The ending doesn't exist. Endings, resolution, and closure are for healthy people and none of the characters in this story are healthy. They are broken and searching for something. Your role is to hope they find it.

In a twist of events SELENE finds herself pinned to the door, aware of the people bustling behind it, wondering if they can see her through the tiny win-dow. AARON leans forward and hesitates, but he is all dark skin and teeth, sad eyes and smirking. SELENE grits through her teeth, you wouldn't dare. *& AARON takes a second, gripping her shoulders and pressing his entire body into her, so she can feel everything—so he can feel everything. SELENE holds her breath. This could be the moment, the first press of flesh against flesh; the air is salty and thick with sweat and silence. AARON backs away, leaving a frenzied SELENE against the door alone.*

Tell me about the first time you said, "I love you," and I'll trade you mine. It's anticlimactic and forced, taking place spontaneously on a lazy afternoon from a distance. I'll let you in on a secret: I didn't say it first, which is why this moment is important. That he wouldn't continue his day until I said it back and once I did, I knew I didn't mean it, I mean, I know I didn't believe it, I mean, I knew that loving him would splinter me like a supernova and I wasn't much of a risk-taker and he was all risk with only the potential of sweet reward—I didn't know. Tell me yours, I'll tell you mine. But swear you won't laugh. When I finally professed my love, he gloated and hindsight tells me I should've known then, but like I said, I knew the first time, I mean, I knew before he even existed, I mean, the feeling in my bones told me that nothing good could come from mutable love. The first time I said it, he told me how so many girls had said it to him before, but he only said it back to one—how good a lie tastes in the ears of a romantic, silky like chocolate, bubbly like champagne, tangy as lemons. Everything I wanted to hear went unsaid, all of it implied in teeth and seductive tones.

When a fire burns, the air has one agenda and the
flame has another. So when AARON put his lips on
SELENE he intended to map her skin with his tongue,
making sure to taste every nook and cranny, every
crevice and plane. SELENE moves slow. SELENE
knows better. SELENE wants to know who decides
their bottom lip gets to be sucked & why there's not
enough air in her chest & why her panties are wet &
who is in control anymore & why AARON is roam-
ing his hands & breath all over her & what happens if
she gives into him & is this the spark & now that it's
here will this hunger ever dwindle & AARON is press-
ing his body into her & SELENE considers melting
or disappearing or permeating or evolving or dying
or living or burning whatever it takes to become this
feeling. AARON pauses, searching for something in
SELENE & she takes this moment as a sign to breathe
to leave to untangle flesh & AARON blinks realizing he
is alone again in the darkness.

Tell me about the spark, the catalyst, that made you know
he was the one, and I'll trade you mine. Was yours slow and
steady? Mine was chaotic. Mine was planets falling off their
axes and lightning causing prairies to burst into flames. Mine
was a blood moon. A free fall. Mine was a path plastered with
bright yellow triangle signage and I just kept walking towards
the warm glow of light. Tell me yours, I'll tell you mine. But
vow you won't steal it for a poem. I say mine, but I mean his,
I mean, we both came to a fork in the road and went opposite
directions, I mean, I couldn't really tell what was happening
in his brain, but fuck I knew how to read the body and the

body said yes, the body said please, the body said I need you right here with me and the body was warm and I was freezing out in the world by myself. He would roam the streets and come back to my bed my body and I mistook that for power. He needed an audience and I fell into the role—I practiced every role; I was understudy for every role. I was provider lover comforter friend mentor teacher student sub dom tease earth fire water air—I lied. Didn't I tell you this is not a love story? There is no such thing as a spark, only demand and supply.

SELENE knows that at some point she will have to sacrifice something to AARON be it blood, dignity, or life. & today SELENE is sacrificing dignity for pleasure. Today SELENE is making herself refreshing pool of water lush meadow grove ripe plump fruit crisp cool air. Today SELENE is transforming her body into a space for AARON's sweet release. HER mouth is where it begins: hot bed of saliva taste buds and hairless skin. AARON is a body of bouncing cells chaotic nerves frenzied hormones frying neurotransmitters. AARON closes his eyes and imagines SELENE as all mouth tongue & throat as warm cozy home as happy place. SELENE purrs with HIM in HER mouth & AARON doesn't know how much he can take if SELENE moves this slow. SELENE is intentional. SELENE is novice making work as practiced. SELENE tastes AARON & swallows what he gives HER without hesitation because AARON is elsewhere AARON is on another plane AARON is all that matters & SELENE is here as paramour bitter and flushed wet and warm.

Tell me about the first time you made love, and I'll trade you mine. I'll bet you had roses or chocolate or there was something gentle and soft or you both poured forth with ecstasy and it brought you closer. Or maybe yours was just as villainous as mine. Disney princesses didn't teach me how to fuck. I learned that from reading and various pornos, and even then, it is a talent to deceive with breathing and moaning and fucking. It is a talent to allow yourself to be vulnerable and surrender your ego to someone else. Tell me yours, I'll tell you mine. But promise you won't be disappointed. There is nothing exciting about our first time besides inevitability, obligation, and betrayal. It was not *our* first time, but only mine because I waited because who else because why not because of him because I wanted because a spark because of timing because I needed because it was there because he needed because he knew because everything the planets did in our favor required a flesh sacrifice and that could only be me. I told you this isn't a love story, or maybe it is, but it's a story between two people who needed something easy and kind, two people who needed to practice, two people who had time, two people losing control, two people who spent a lot of energy crafting ways to cast human into pet: doting and loyal. This is a story about everything going wrong.

SELENE and AARON are no stranger to silence. Sometimes THEY sit in the same room and say little, minds already a cacophony of voices emotions & insecurity. SELENE and AARON talk the most when they are doing mundane things. AARON likes to walk with SELENE, making sure she stands on the side furthest from the street, keeping pace with her slow

and carefree stride, listening to her rattle off infor-
mation anxieties questions & curiosities without feel-
ing judged. AARON loves the way her voice lilts and
caresses his ears gently, loves the way it climbs into
a soprano when she's excited, loves the bass in her
laugh. SELENE likes to watch AARON work, studying
the way he furrows his brow or becomes absorbed by
the line on the page. HIS devotion to learning some-
thing new is inspiring is distraction is what makes
SELENE want to become unknown or reimagined, just
to be discovered by HIM again. SHE loves to watch
his lips as HE talks about passions and fall into the
depths of his eyes, hoping maybe one day SHE will be
able to explore the nooks and crannies of his brain the
way THEY do their bodies.

Tell me about the last time you said, "I love you," and I'll trade you mine. Was it last night? This morning? Right now? The word is unfamiliar on my tongue, bitter and unbelievable, burnt and inedible. It would be too romantic to tell you that my last time was my first time, and also a lie. But imagine the string of spit hanging between two people who both knew it was over as they licked their lips after a final kiss of gratitude: thank you for giving me your body thank you for taking me to a new dimension thank you for opening thank you for filling me thank you for satiating my desire thank you for replacing my depression with something concrete and measurable thank you for what I believe was love thank you for this moment thank you for this memory thank you but we don't need each other anymore. When a supernova implodes it puts on a brilliant display that only reaches the human eye as a twinkle.

Tell me who's the villain, I'll tell you the truth. Swear to never tell a soul. There are no heroes here, no one to root for. I have tried for years to detach myself from the damsel from the virgin from the bamboozled. I am none of those things. I am the inverse of those things. I knew that love couldn't exist between the broken. I knew I didn't love him at first and I knew he didn't love me at last. I knew that timing was inconsequential. I knew neither of us knew what we needed—but still these are all assumptions, all implied words in silences and distances, there is no way for me to ever know what happens at the end. This is not a love story, but an interlude.

The last time they are together, SELENE drinks a little too much tequila and orange juice & does a bunch of stupid angry things. SHE is leaving the place she loves—she is losing what she loves. AARON helps her organize her clothes into her suitcase, rolling them compactly. When HE is out of the room, SELENE quickly slips on his boots and flexes her toes. This is her secret. AARON sits on the bed, watching SELENE empty her dresser tucked underneath, bobbing between his legs to reach the drawers. SHE works in silence. The air is heavy, electric; one right word right gesture right exhale could set the room on fire. When they leave, SELENE and AARON sit in the backseat of the car & SELENE puts her head on AARON'S shoulder, leaning into him as she falls into a tipsy slumber, breathing softly. AARON keeps his right arm completely still the whole way up & everything feels right for the both of them: sad and sensitive planets aligned unknowing on the horizon.

are you so damn hesitant? I'll return the favor, later. I want all of it. I know what you want. I know what you like. You don't have to sw...
Just let me… I want to fuck you. I've always wanted to be with a darkskinned girl. I'm not even all the way in. Suck them like you wou...
e just going to leave me with blue balls? Sit here for a minute. I'd fuck her all the time, all day, everyday – she wouldn't even hav...
ith a white guy. You're kind of loud. I know you like it. Sexy. Can I take them off? I missed you. You can spit it out. Bend over...
your tits? Let me see. The face you make. Your turn. Come here. Don't talk like that. Wait… Please? I know. I'm trying. Ta...
moaning all loud and shit. How many times? Look, I'm soft now. May I? Can I? You took too long. See what you've done to me…
elf? Almost. I wanted to come. You're so tight. Spread your legs. Put your leg up. Yes… Just like that… Make it wet. Are yo...
mouth do? I heard you were good. Don't pretend you're innocent. Don't stop. Faster. Shit. Fuck. Tell me you like it. Oo...
Get on top. You came. I came. I'm gonna come. Do you want the balls? Do you want th... I bet that pussy's murdered people. Why are you so damn hesitant? I'll return the favor, later. I want all of it. I kno...
have to swallow. Shhh… You're so wet. Just let me… I want to fuck you. I've always wanted to be with a darkskinne...
ou would a dick. Two fingers? Four? You're just going to leave me with blue balls? Sit here for a minute. I'd fuck b...
have to exercise. You should have sex with a white guy. You're kind of loud. I know you li...
Get on top. Is that blood? Can I hold your tits? Let me see. The face you make. Y...
your bra off. Right now. You were moaning all loud and s... How many ti...
Show me. Why don't you touch yourself? Almost. I wante...
ady? You can feel that? What that mouth do? I heard you w... gonna come. Do you want th...
...efore. See, when you talk like that… I bet that pussy's murdered people. Why are you so damn he...
...ant. I know what you like. You don't have to swallow. Shhh… You're so wet. Just let me… I...
...ot even all the way in. Suck them like you would a dick. Two fingers? Four? You're just goin...
me, all day, everyday – she wouldn't even have to exercise. You should have sex with a white g...
I missed you. You can spit it out. Bend over. Get on top. Is that blood? Can I hold your tits? I...
Wait… Please? I know. I'm trying. Take your bra off. Right now. You were moaning all loud...
ook too long. See what you've done to me? Show me. Why don't you touch yourself? Almost. I wa...
es… Just like that… Make it wet. Are you ready? You can feel that? What that mouth do? I heard yo...
. Shit. Fuck. Tell me you like it. Oops. Ouch. You don't have sex a lot do you? You came. I...
e your stress. I've never been with a big girl before. See, when you talk like that… I bet that pussy's murde...
vor, later. I want all of it. I know what you want. I know what you like. You don't have to swallow. Shhh…
s wanted to be with a darkskinned girl. I'm not even all the way in. Suck them like you would a dick.
. Sit here for a minute. I'd fuck her all the time, all day, everyday – she wouldn't even have to exercise. You're kind of
w you like it. Sexy. Can I take them off? I missed you. You can spit it out. Bend over. Can I hold your tits? Let me see. The fac...
. Your turn. Come here. Don't talk like that. Wait. Please? I know. I'm trying. Take your bra off. Right now. You were moaning all loud and shit. How

FOR YOUR PLEASURE

IN GRADUATE SCHOOL, I TOOK A "WRITING SEX" **CLASS,** during which we read a lot of books about white people having intercourse or contemplating their sexuality, and we looked at a lot of art of white bodies. And it was while looking at one of these pieces, a self-portrait of a woman masturbating, and listening to my classmate swear under her breath at the image, that I realized: There would be no images of black bodies in this curriculum.

And the class became its most interesting when I realized we would never look at a black body. Now sure, we read a couple narratives by queer people of color. But we didn't look at any images of black people in sexual situations. I wasn't represented in my class. I couldn't relate to any of the materials. I developed a disdain for writing about sex and erotica. One night, I wrote this sentence: "The black body is so sexualized, it can't even be taught." So, like any rebellious creative-writing-slash-art student, I carved my own space. For my final project, I decided to create a hybrid piece in order to analyze my sex life and get to the root of why certain men choose to objectify me—a fat black woman—without even knowing me.

I began with a catalog. What had men—lovers, friends, acquaintances, strangers—said to me when they were thinking with their dicks instead of their brains? Why, or how, could a man look at me and believe it was appropriate to say exactly what they were thinking? What is it about my body that makes me devourable, if not desirable? So, I started writing down every outlandish thing a man had ever said to me in the heat of the moment, when flirting, or trying to get into my pants.

I said, "Curiosity killed the cat," and he responded with: "I bet that pussy's murdered people."

I am doing dishes after a party and a man stands behind me and whispers, "I've never been with a big girl before."

My friend tells me that sex with a dark-skinned girl is on his bucket list.

My lover thinks that I should have more sex, specifically with white men.

A man from Tinder messaged me every night at 2 a.m. that I should come over and put him to sleep with my mouth.

My reaction was always shock, slight annoyance, or amusement. Shock because why are you saying that to me? Annoyance because no, I don't want to actually do anything with or for you. Amusement because oh, someone thinks I'm pretty, someone thinks I have sex appeal.

I never learned about sex and blackness together. Black sexuality is not a concept in education. Sex-ed posters are always of white bodies with average genitalia, palms supine. So, I learned about sex by reading everything and anything I could get my hands on. Biology and anatomy books, coming-of-age and adult fiction, books by therapists and psychologists—but I didn't learn anything about black sexuality. It's difficult for non-black people to tackle subjects of black sex because of the thin line between offensive and educational. We can blame slavery for that. The whole black people are sexually deviant beasts and will seduce white men and assault white women thing, when really, the opposite was occurring. But growing up, it was even more difficult for me to form a sexual identity when my mother wouldn't talk about it, and one of my cousins called me Jezebel, and pornography starring black actors and actresses seemed to be filmed with a fetishistic and aggressive gaze. Black sexuality is complicated.

But these men were telling me these things and I relished the attention, so I engaged and indulged. I didn't know any better. But I did know that I wanted to be wanted, necessary, desirable. I had the simple goal of being attractive and attracting a man. I was reckless. And at some point, my reckless indulgence morphed into submission, and my submission morphed into masochism, and these relationships were going nowhere, and I was receding further and further into myself, losing my body to the hands and mouths of men.

Eventually, my body was not my own.

...ILL TELL YOU THE TRUTH ABOUT HAVING SEX. I LIKE SEX I DO, BUT PART

...RNEATH YOU, BELIEVING THAT YOU ARE SO INTO MY BODY, YOU'VE FORG

...EETS, SINKING SO DEEP INTO MY MATTRESS THAT I AM NOTHING MORE

...UR NEED. I HATED MYSELF SO MUCH. I SCREAMED DEEPER! DEEPER! HOPIN

...ACKING MY BONES, SPLITTING MY SKIN. I DON'T THINK I WAS WISHING F

...ANTED ME TO SEE ME. I WILL TELL YOU THE TRUTH ABOUT HAVING SEX.

...E BEING PINNED UNDERNEATH YOU, BELIEVING THAT YOU ARE SO INTO

...T, SINKING INTO THE SHEETS, SINKING SO DEEP INTO MY MATTRESS THAT

...BODY; I RELISHED YOUR NEED. I HATED MYSELF SO MUCH. I SCREAMEI

...IN HALF FROM THE HIPS: CRACKING MY BONES, SPLITTING MY SKIN. I DO

...U TO SEE ME – OR MAYBE I WANTED ME TO SEE ME. I WILL TELL YOU THE

...SOCHISTIC PLEASURE. I LIKE BEING PINNED UNDERNEATH YOU, BELIEVIN

...KING INTO THE BLANKET, SINKING INTO THE SHEETS, SINKING SO DEEP

...ATH YOU. YOU NEEDED MY BODY; I RELISHED YOUR NEED. I HATED M

...EPLY, IT WOULD TEAR ME IN HALF FROM THE HIPS: CRACKING MY BONES

...UNDS. I JUST WANTED YOU TO SEE ME – OR MAYBE I WANTED ME TO SEE

...JOYMENT OF SEX IS A MASOCHISTIC PLEASURE. I LIKE BEING PINNED UN

...THERE. I FEEL MYSELF SINKING INTO THE BLANKET, SINKING INTO THE SH

...D THE SPRINGS BENEATH YOU. YOU NEEDED MY BODY; I RELISHED YOUR

...OULD THRUST SO DEEPLY, IT WOULD TEAR ME IN HALF FROM THE HIPS: CR

...T THAT'S HOW IT SOUNDS. I JUST WANTED YOU TO SEE ME – OR MAYBE

..., BUT PART OF MY ENJOYMENT OF SEX IS A MASOCHISTIC PLEASURE. I LI

...U'VE FORGOTTEN I AM THERE. I FEEL MYSELF SINKING INTO THE BLANKET

...G MORE THAN **PUSSY** AND THE SPRINGS BENEATH YOU. YOU NEEDED M

...EPER! HOPING THAT YOU WOULD THRUST SO DEEPLY, IT WOULD TEAR ME

...S WISHING FOR DEATH, BUT THAT'S HOW IT SOUNDS. I JUST WANTED YOU

...VING SEX. I LIKE SEX I DO, BUT PART OF MY ENJOYMENT OF SEX IS A MASO

...E SO INTO MY BODY, YOU'VE FORGOTTEN I AM THERE. I FEEL MYSELF SINK

...ESS THAT I AM NOTHING MORE THAN **PUSSY** AND THE SPRINGS BENEATH

...REAMED DEEPER! DEEPER! HOPING THAT YOU WOULD THRUST SO DEEPLY

...N. I DON'T THINK I WAS WISHING FOR DEATH, BUT THAT'S HOW IT SOUNT

...U THE TRUTH ABOUT HAVING SEX. I LIKE SEX I DO, BUT PART OF MY ENJOY

...IEVING THAT YOU ARE SO INTO MY BODY, YOU'VE FORGOTTEN I AM THE

...DEEP INTO MY MATTRESS THAT I AM NOTHING MORE THAN PUSSY AND

...MYSELF SO MUCH. I SCREAMED DEEPER! DEEPER! HOPING THAT YOU WOU

...NES, SPLITTING MY SKIN. I DON'T THINK I WAS WISHING FOR DEATH, BUT T

...ME. I WILL TELL YOU THE TRUTH ABOUT HAVING SEX. I LIKE SEX I DO, BUT

...DERNEATH YOU, BELIEVING THAT YOU ARE SO INTO MY BODY, YOU'VE FOI

...EETS, SINKING SO DEEP INTO MY MATTRESS THAT I AM NOTHING MORE THA

...ED. I HATED MYSELF SO MUCH. I SCREAMED DEEPER! DEEPER! HOPING THA

NJOYMENT OF SEX IS A MASOCHISTIC PLEASURE. I LIKE BEING PINNED U
AM THERE. I FEEL MYSELF SINKING INTO THE BLANKET, SINKING INTO T
SSY AND THE SPRINGS BENEATH YOU. YOU NEEDED MY BODY; I RELISH
OU WOULD THRUST SO DEEPLY, IT WOULD TEAR ME IN HALF FROM THE HI
H, BUT THAT'S HOW IT SOUNDS. I JUST WANTED YOU TO SEE ME – OR MAY
X I DO, BUT PART OF MY ENJOYMENT OF SEX IS A MASOCHISTIC PLEASUR
Y, YOU'VE FORGOTTEN I AM THERE. I FEEL MYSELF SINKING INTO THE BLA
OTHING MORE THAN **PUSSY** AND THE SPRINGS BENEATH YOU. YOU NEED
R! DEEPER! HOPING THAT YOU WOULD THRUST SO DEEPLY, IT WOULD TE
NK I WAS WISHING FOR DEATH, BUT THAT'S HOW IT SOUNDS. I JUST WANT
BOUT HAVING SEX. I LIKE SEX I DO, BUT PART OF MY ENJOYMENT OF SEX I
YOU ARE SO INTO MY BODY, YOU'VE FORGOTTEN I AM THERE. I FEEL MYSE
MATTRESS THAT I AM NOTHING MORE THAN **PUSSY** AND THE SPRINGS
UCH, I SCREAMED DEEPER! DEEPER! HOPING THAT YOU WOULD THRUST
G MY SKIN. I DON'T THINK I WAS WISHING FOR DEATH, BUT THAT'S HOW
TELL YOU THE TRUTH ABOUT HAVING SEX. I LIKE SEX I DO, BUT PART OF
H YOU, BELIEVING THAT YOU ARE SO INTO MY BODY, YOU'VE FORGOTTE
NKING SO DEEP INTO MY MATTRESS THAT I AM NOTHING MORE THAN **PUS**
HATED MYSELF SO MUCH. I SCREAMED DEEPER! DEEPER! HOPING THAT Y
MY BONES, SPLITTING MY SKIN. I DON'T THINK I WAS WISHING FOR DEA
ME TO SEE ME. I WILL TELL YOU THE TRUTH ABOUT HAVING SEX. I LIKE SE
PINNED UNDERNEATH YOU, BELIEVING THAT YOU ARE SO INTO MY BO
INTO THE SHEETS, SINKING SO DEEP INTO MY MATTRESS THAT I AM NOT
I RELISHED YOUR NEED. I HATED MYSELF SO MUCH. I SCREAMED DEEP
FROM THE HIPS: CRACKING MY BONES, SPLITTING MY SKIN. I DON'T THIN
ME – OR MAYBE I WANTED ME TO SEE ME. I WILL TELL YOU THE TRUTH ABO
S PLEASURE. I LIKE BEING PINNED UNDERNEATH YOU, BELIEVING THAT Y
O THE BLANKET, SINKING INTO THE SHEETS, SINKING SO DEEP INTO MY M
OU NEEDED MY BODY; I RELISHED YOUR NEED. I HATED MYSELF SO MUCI
LD TEAR ME IN HALF FROM THE HIPS: CRACKING MY BONES, SPLITTING
WANTED YOU TO SEE ME – OR MAYBE I WANTED ME TO SEE ME. I WILL TE
E SEX IS A MASOCHISTIC PLEASURE. I LIKE BEING PINNED UNDERNEATH YO
L MYSELF SINKING INTO THE BLANKET, SINKING INTO THE SHEETS, SINKI
NGS BENEATH YOU. YOU NEEDED MY BODY; I RELISHED YOUR NEED. I H
UST SO DEEPLY, IT WOULD TEAR ME IN HALF FROM THE HIPS: CRACKING
OW IT SOUNDS. I JUST WANTED YOU TO SEE ME – OR MAYBE I WANTED ME
F MY ENJOYMENT OF SEX IS A MASOCHISTIC PLEASURE. I LIKE BEING PINN
N I AM THERE. I FEEL MYSELF SINKING INTO THE BLANKET, SINKING INTO T
Y AND THE SPRINGS BENEATH YOU. YOU NEEDED MY BODY; I RELISHED YO
OULD THRUST SO DEEPLY, IT WOULD TEAR ME IN HALF FROM THE HIPS: CR

I've thought of all the ways to describe what my body was to them—what I was to them. Because I was not a person, I knew that. I knew that I was a "what" and not a "who." I was sex doll. Sex toy. Orifice. Pleasure. Urge. Challenge. Trash. Nothing. Fetish.

After cataloging everything I could remember men saying to me, I tried to write about the encounters that formed my sexual identity. Outside of the books and films, how did I learn about sex and everything else that led up to it? There was the stranger on World of Warcraft paying my character to dance, so he could masturbate behind his computer screen. That was technically the first time I ever made a man come. There was my best friend explaining the difference between sex and oral sex to me in eighth grade on the playground. Until then, I had thought it just meant kissing. And each memory dredged up a sickening feeling in me, like I shouldn't have so many experiences and encounters to pull from, like each one added to the reality of my thesis of the black body being over-sexualized.

To avoid that feeling, I only wrote about the body in second person. It was easier for me to disassociate from my own body and force my feelings onto the reader. You will be used by these men you love. You will hate yourself. You will understand the difference between love and lust, walking with a beam and no harness on the tightrope between them. You will fall. In second person, your hands become mine, and you have to feel it, you have to empathize with all that pain and confusion—or you reject it. You don't like the piece. You don't get it. It made you uncomfortable.

Each time I sat down to write about my own objectification, my stomach clenched, and anxiety bloomed in my chest—I would be staring at the computer screen triggering myself and wondering, why didn't I do anything?

I never had an answer.

Maybe it was love, maybe it was curiosity, maybe it was masochism.

It was easier, instead, to focus on the men in these encounters, imagining their perspectives when interacting with me: what they saw, how they spoke, when they licked their lips, what was behind their stares, how it felt when they touched me. I constructed these experiences into scenes, directions, and roles to be filled. I wanted people who engaged with the project to only have two choices: objectify or be objectified. You empathized with them or me—my voice existing as object and narrator, with no way of knowing what was happening below the surface.

After I had the words and the encounters, I knew I had to put myself into the project—or rather my body. I was exploring objectification, and so I needed to become an object, literally. My body became part of the project that you could fit right into—regardless of shape, size, or identity—I knew what it's like to be hunted, I knew what it's like to be powerless, I knew what it's like to encounter someone who treated me as less than. In order to make myself an object, I was forced to objectify myself in the process. It was exhausting. I printed my body onto paper, took photos of myself in sexual positions, traced every line of my body on the computer, spent hours in the lab exporting my body into vector files, I had my body laser-cut onto acrylic, onto paper, so I was now a tangible thing that could be held in the palm of my hand—wondering the entire time, what is so desirable about this shape, what are men getting out of this, what am I getting out of this?

For Writing Sex class, I made prints and let people hold the acrylic sheets of my bodies: translucent in their hands. My classmates passing my body around the room for critique and commentary. I titled my project *For Your Pleasure.* And *For Your Pleasure* became an ongoing piece that existed after the class had ended, after the semester had been completed, and still grows with each epiphany or encounter that I have.

The project became a gallery exhibition, and I stood anxiously in a room while people walked around staring at my body on the walls, reading various moments of objectification, and all I wanted to know was what they were thinking. I ate cake. I wished that the cake decorators could have put my body on the cake, so people would be forced to literally consume me. I mingled with visitors. At one point, I danced and sang to the carefully curated playlist of black women singing about objectification and mistaken love. Sometimes, I wasn't in the gallery, and people were putting these Post-its on the wall, which let me know a little about what they were thinking—but how did it feel to be a body in a space covered with bodies? How did it feel to read the things men said to me, the ways they used language to morph me into only a body? How did it feel to have the walls talking to you, performing for you; to have the art accosting you—to be unwillingly cast into a role you never asked for?

Me too.

I wanted people to feel uncomfortable. I wanted them to be conflicted about enjoying the art. I wanted them to feel like they were constantly being objectified within the space, while also being an objectifier. I wanted them to take these cut-outs of me and throw them away, cut them up, fold their gum, drop them, etc., and understand objectification. Forty-three days later, I painted over every single silhouette and word in white. It took me and two friends, a day and a half, about fifteen hours. It was the literal erasure I have always understood happens to black women and our work. The same erasure of humanity in objectification. Underneath that blank acrylic slate is a woman. My shoulders ached. My jumpsuit, hair, face, and palms were covered in white paint. I wondered how I could write about the body after all of it.

A few days after *For Your Pleasure* had opened in the gallery space, the man from Tinder asked when I would "come see him" next, which really meant, when is the next time we would fuck, and I told him that I was not in the mood for sex. But really, I was not in the mood to be objectified, to push myself far away from the situation while my body still performed for him. I was not in the mood to devote the effort necessary to being someone else's source of pleasure. He said he understood. I didn't really believe him. I found out later, that either that day or the next day or the one after, that it was his birthday, and part of me felt obligated to give him my body as a gift, knowing there would be no "thank you" or appreciation afterwards. But we didn't know each other like that. And now, we don't talk, which is typically how these encounters go.

When I look at *For Your Pleasure*, I think of how far I've come and how far I still have to go. There are so many encounters waiting to be unearthed from inside me and resurrected on the page. These are fragments from the flip side of the project, side B if you will, where I explored and tried to make sense of what was happening with my body and how I was interacting with those men.

I knew I was an object, because an object is necessary. Like water or food or air, there's only so long someone can go without. And I didn't object to this objectification. Before I was an object, I had never been necessary. I had never been noticed. I had never had a presence. And I had spent years mistaking nothing for love, which splintered me into pieces, like steak neatly sliced for plating. So, I was plated into the lives of various men who couldn't care less if I were there or not. And as they consumed my energy, my intellect, my time, and my love, I felt myself disappearing. And I was okay with that because part of me longed to know what it felt like to be nothing.

Could this be mutual objectification? You want me for the satisfaction of orgasm without consequences, without guilt. I want you for the satisfaction of bringing you to orgasm. I want to watch you morph into your most vulnerable. I want to swallow that vulnerability; I want to drain your power. And I want to do it all without you even touching me. I want you to believe I don't need you even as my body screams otherwise. Can you hear me? What does desire sound like? It feels like being ripped in half, one leg in each direction.

Creating with the body—your body, my body—requires distance, sacrifice. You've got to be willing to dive into those trenches you've dug within yourself to get the emotion necessary to produce something of value. Sometimes it's triggering. Sometimes it's enlightening. I haven't found a way to write about the body—my body—without objectifying myself or quitting. I still don't feel like it's completely mine. I've been asking myself the same question for what seems like forever, "How do I reclaim my body?"

And so far, the only answer I've come up with is time.

BECAUSE IT FELT SO GOOD WHEN I HATED MYSELF TO AT LEAST PRETEND THAT I WAS IN LOVE. BECAUSE IT FELT SO GOOD WHEN I HATED MYSELF TO BELIEVE THAT I WAS BEAUTIFUL. BECAUSE IT FELT SO GOOD WHEN I HATED MYSELF TO THINK THAT I WAS WORTH SOMETHING. BECAUSE IT FELT SO GOOD WHEN I HATED MYSELF TO HAVE SOMETHING INSIDE OF ME. BECAUSE IT FELT SO GOOD WHEN I HATED MYSELF TO THINK THAT I HAD MORE TO GIVE. BECAUSE IT FELT SO GOOD WHEN I HATED MYSELF TO GIVE MYSELF AWAY TO THE UNDERSERVING. BECAUSE IT FELT SO GOOD WHEN I HATED MYSELF TO KNOW WHAT LIPS TASTED LIKE. BECAUSE IT FELT SO GOOD WHEN I HATED MYSELF TO FEEL ANOTHER PERSON'S WARMTH. BECAUSE IT FELT SO GOOD WHEN I HATED MYSELF TO SINK INTO THE SHEETS, THE WALL, THE GROUND. BECAUSE IT FELT SO GOOD WHEN I HATED MYSELF TO DISAPPEAR INTO ANOTHER PERSON'S PRIMAL URGES. BECAUSE IT FELT SO GOOD WHEN I HATED MYSELF TO HEAR THE WORD LOVE. BECAUSE IT FELT SO GOOD WHEN I HATED MYSELF TO THINK SOMEONE LOVED ME. BECAUSE IT FELT SO GOOD WHEN I HATED MYSELF TO BE WANTED. BECAUSE IT FELT SO GOOD WHEN I HATED MYSELF TO FEEL LUSTED. BECAUSE IT FELT SO GOOD WHEN I HATED MYSELF TO THINK SOMEONE CARED ABOUT ME. BECAUSE IT FELT SO GOOD WHEN I HATED MYSELF TO HAVE SOMETHING, ANYTHING. BECAUSE IT FELT SO GOOD WHEN I HATED MYSELF TO AT LEAST PRETEND THAT I WAS IN LOVE. BECAUSE IT FELT SO GOOD WHEN I HATED MYSELF TO BELIEVE THAT I WAS BEAUTIFUL. BECAUSE IT FELT SO GOOD WHEN I HATED MYSELF TO THINK THAT I WAS WORTH SOMETHING. BECAUSE IT FELT SO GOOD WHEN I HATED MYSELF TO HAVE SOMETHING INSIDE OF ME. BECAUSE IT FELT SO GOOD WHEN I HATED MYSELF TO FILL THAT VOID WITH SEX. BECAUSE IT FELT SO GOOD WHEN I HATED MYSELF TO KNOW WHAT LIPS TASTED LIKE. BECAUSE IT FELT SO GOOD WHEN I HATED MYSELF TO SINK INTO THE SHEETS, THE WALL, THE GROUND. BECAUSE IT FELT SO GOOD WHEN I HATED MYSELF TO HEAR THE WORD LOVE. BECAUSE IT FELT SO GOOD WHEN I HATED MYSELF TO FEEL ANOTHER PERSON'S WARMTH. BECAUSE IT FELT SO GOOD WHEN I HATED MYSELF TO FILL THAT VOID WITH SEX. BECAUSE IT FELT SO GOOD WHEN I HATED MYSELF TO HEAR THE WORD LOVE. BECAUSE IT FELT SO GOOD WHEN I HATED MYSELF TO FEEL LUSTED. BECAUSE IT FELT SO GOOD WHEN I HATED MYSELF TO DISAPPEAR INTO ANOTHER PERSON'S PRIMAL URGES. BECAUSE IT FELT SO GOOD WHEN I HATED MYSELF TO GIVE MYSELF AWAY TO THE UNDERSERVING. BECAUSE IT FELT SO GOOD WHEN I HATED MYSELF TO HAVE SOMETHING, ANYTHING. BECAUSE IT FELT SO GOOD WHEN I HATED MYSELF TO BELIEVE THAT I WAS BEAUTIFUL. BECAUSE IT FELT SO GOOD WHEN I HATED MYSELF TO THINK THAT I WAS WORTH SOMETHING. BECAUSE IT FELT SO GOOD WHEN I HATED MYSELF. BECAUSE IT FELT SO GOOD WHEN I HATED MYSELF. BECAUSE IT FELT SO GOOD WHEN I HATED MYSELF. BECAUSE IT FELT SO GOOD WHEN I HATED MYSELF. BECAUSE IT FELT SO GOOD WHEN I HATED MYSELF. BECAUSE IT FELT SO GOOD WHEN I HATED MYSELF. BECAUSE IT FELT SO GOOD WHEN I HATED MYSELF. BECAUSE IT FELT SO GOOD WHEN I HATED MYSELF. BECAUSE IT FELT SO GOOD. BECAUSE IT FELT SO GOOD. BECAUSE IT FELT SO GOOD. BECAUSE IT FELT SO GOOD. BECAUSE IT FELT SO GOOD. BECAUSE IT FELT SO GOOD. BECAUSE IT FELT SO GOOD. BECAUSE IT FELT SO GOOD. BECAUSE IT FELT SO GOOD. BECAUSE IT FELT SO GOOD. BECAUSE IT FELT SO GOOD. BECAUSE IT FELT SO GOOD. BECAUSE IT FELT SO GOOD. BECAUSE IT FELT SO GOOD. BECAUSE IT FELT SO GOOD TO BE AN OBJECT, TO NOT EXIST.

MARGINALIA

Black (adj.):   *very darkest color*
absence   complete absorption of light;   opposite
of white;   *dark col-*
ored skin   *African*
     ancestry;
                    tragic   disastrous   ;
despair   pessimism

I've been thinking about ways I can force myself onto the page. I have considered the following: bleeding onto it, gluing a strand of hair or a scab, licking it, spitting on it, wiping the oils from my face with it, crying onto it—

I have decided: I want to ingest it.

I will show this page that it's nothing without me. Nothing but a blank space to be abused, manipulated, caressed, thrown away, recycled, stained. Nothing without me.

I've forgotten the definition of the adjective that I use to identify myself: black.

I should capitalize it: Black.

A self-portrait:

You can't see me because I am an absence.
Quite possibly, I've absorbed you, the light—
What is it that you want me to say?
Are you afraid that I'll rub off on you?

I'm simply trying to carve an existence onto the page that doesn't require me to remain in the margins. They say my work and I are marginalized, and yet, here I am, very literally using the space?

It must be a hyperbole. This is all hyperbole. Am I a hyperbole?

No, I am arguing for my presence. The Black body in the room, unavoidable, yet censored.

Is this an argument, a confession, or a prayer?

I've realized that Black art can't only be interesting, can't lack charisma, can't be too abstract, can't meander, can't be shitty, can't can't can't can't can't. Female art can't be too political, can't be apolitical, can't be too pretty, can't be shitty, can't can't can't can't can't. Marginalized work can't be shitty, can't can't can't can't can't can't—oppressed people's art must be innovative, must resonate.

I don't know if my argument is working.

You will not white-wash my existence. You will not white-wash my work. You will not white-wash my existence. You will not white-wash my work. You will not white-wash my existence. You will not white-wash my work. You will not white-wash my existence. You will not white-wash my work. You will not white-wash my existence. You will not white-wash—

You will not white-wash me.

I'm beginning to think that the page may require a blood sacrifice or something more—a body? Just so I can be heard, if not understood.

Can a page be hallowed ground? Can a song be hallowed ground? After I ingested the paper, its edges cut me all the way down my throat, and I wondered, should I waste my time on a craft that's betraying me, no, resisting me?

My crisis is that my space, the page, has been compromised. They took it from me without my permission. Stripped my worth from the page. Left me with its shredded remains.

Why did you take it away from me?

Where am I supposed to go?

I used to feel safe here; the page used to be my home.

This was the only place I wasn't silenced.

They're trying to kill me, are you they?

I only ask for a funeral pyre. Use this essay to hold the flame.

You cannot erase me.

I wonder if I should also try to ingest the pen, if that will be enough to prove that my work is worth something. But, if I swallow the pen, should I drink the ink first, blacken my teeth, tongue, and gums?

Am I not Black enough for you?

Nothing blacker than heritage—maybe blood.

I've never wanted to be white. It's never appealed to me, and I think that's because I've been forced to learn several different versions of history, each coinciding with an identity: USA/"American" (white), Black (African-American), women's (feminism/womanism). I've been forced to learn the vernaculars of each space, the behaviors of its peoples—I've been forced to look at most things objectively to understand how a white man thinks.

It's the twenty-first century and white people are still out here screaming, "We're all immigrants!"

Is that how you perceive the indigenous people of a colonized land?

Is that how you perceive the great-great-great-great-grandchildren of a stolen people, no claim to any land?

Displacement.

This is my last attempt. I sink down onto my knees to pray—

I need you to understand that I am not soft.

I am hard like diamond; mined like diamond—

at my core, there is an entire history of suffering and oppression that resulted in my existence.

WHAT WILL FOLLOW

MY DAD IS DEAD. I can hear it in the panicked tone my mom is using to speak into her phone, even though she won't tell us. Instead of taking us to dinner, she drops my sister and me off at a family friend's house and we play cards and bake cookies before going to our school's elementary-wide talent performance, the Extravaganza. Tonight is the end of a lot of things. This is the last Extravaganza that my music teacher will take part in and I will never forget the way she clicks her ruby red slippers at the end of the show to remind us all she is moving to Kansas. I don't know it yet, but this is also my last Extravaganza. Next year, in fourth grade, I will eat too many clementines, get sick, and have to stay home. Tonight, my sister and I will lose a parent and our family will shrink.

Before all of this though, my mom has to drive from the hospital to pick us up from her friend's house after the Extravaganza. She has to sit in the car and listen as we tell her about the amateur acrobatics we performed and the songs we sang. She will put the car in park outside of our house and begin to tell us, but I will interrupt her and say, "He's dead, isn't he?" I will ask where his body is, and she will tell me it's at the hospital and not inside our house where my dad has been dying for months. My sister will cry all night and I will sit on my bed next to her, trying to be a good older sister by looking out of the window without shedding a single tear. I am eight years old.

I will find out by listening in on phone conversations that my half-brother, on my father's side, tried and kept trying: forcing air into our dad's lungs and pressing on his fragile chest even after the paramedics came. In the house, the hospital bed is empty and stripped of its blue sheets and the house is filled with stale air. The hospital will come and remove the bed, the tubes, and the empty bedpan, but they will leave the spare white sheets and clean bed padding, which will be put on the highest shelf of my closet where I won't find them for years.

By choice and fear, I will not attend the visitation. I sit in the backseat of the car alone as my family all go inside to have one final look at his body. I am in the car by myself for a long time, wondering what he looks like, if they've cleaned him up or if he's in his camouflage army uniform for a war I never had the chance to ask about. I wonder if he still has his dreads or if they shaved them all off, including the ones hanging from his chin. I wonder if he still looks like my dad. I wait. They return to the car and my sister, who seems more mature than ever, cups her hand against my ear and whispers, "He looks like he's sleeping."

My mom lets Nia and I stay home from the funeral. We sit on our cousin's faded maroon leather couch while everyone but us and our cousin Ashley attends. Our cousin is peppier than seems appropriate as she talks to another one of her cousins sitting in a faded recliner. My sister and I listen as Ashley talks about how great our dad was, how he was funny and nice, and my sister and I will have nothing to say. It is no longer April 11th, a date now burned onto our brains.

When we go to my dad's house on Leonard Avenue, it doesn't cross my mind that this will be the last time I see my second home. We lived with our mother because our parents never married; sometimes we spent weekends with our dad and sometimes he came over to our house when our mom was gone, taking us to and from school. This is the last time I will see the fallen, forest green siding hanging off the front of the house lit only by red, yellow, and green, Rasta-colored lamplights; and the last time I will walk through the green door with the Ethiopian flag hanging in front. I am allowed to take whatever I want, my mother tells me, and I disregard the bin of toys that my sister and I shared and pick up a golden-framed photo that will never be hung. It is of me as a baby, months old, with my pre-dreadlock afro and dressed in my signature yellow onesie with matching hair bow. My dad is holding me, not looking at the camera, but instead at me as I stare wide-eyed at the camera and most likely my mom behind it. There are a lot of photos like this: he and I, and they're all Polaroids trapped underneath noisy plastic covers in a photo album. But this one is mine. It is one of the few things I take from the house and it will never be my mother's and it will never be my sister's. I don't know what happens to the rest of the items in the house; we left Edward to make those decisions.

On Father's Day, two months after his death when things begin to return to normal, my sister and I stick handmade construction paper Father's Day cards in the back of the framed photo. They sit there for years, fading and unread, and no one bothers to throw them away or move them. Three dates seem to be bolded on the calendar: April 11th, Father's Day, and December 12th. My sister and I work hard to calculate his would-be age every year on December 12th (his birthday), but we don't talk about him. These days come and pass like any other, with an occasional, "Do you know what day it is?" from our mother and a quiet, "Yes" in response.

A year later for spring break, we go to Universal Studios with two of my mother's coworkers and their two daughters, Melanie and Giselle. I am the oldest in the group and my sister is the youngest, and though it will take us a few more years to realize we don't really know or like either of these girls, we think we are friends. We are in the backseat of the rental van, the four of us—three piled in the far back and one of us sitting in the middle row next to one of the other moms.

"You don't know who your daddy is." Melanie states it so bluntly that my sister and I can only look at each other to recover from the shock.

"Yes, we do." We speak in unison and I look from the depths of the backseat towards the front where my mother sits talking to her friends.

"Our dad died." My voice is quiet. They look at me skeptically, ready to laugh.

"What's his name then?" Giselle counters, and the two of them smirk at Nia and me. We are confused because we know exactly who our dad is and have no reason to lie.

"Our daddy is Edward Joseph Gaines." My sister's voice is strong and matter-of-fact even though she is not even seven years old. I look back and forth between Nia, the two girls, and our mothers, who are now eavesdropping on the conversation from their seats.

"That's not your daddy. That's just the man your mom told you was your daddy." Melanie spits her words at us, hot from her seven-year-old mouth. Our mom jumps in and tells them we know our dad and somehow the older women find something to laugh about from our conversation, but Melanie's words sit with me and Nia.

Later, our mom sits us down in the hotel room and tells us that Melanie and Giselle don't know their dads. That their mothers told them that a man was their dad, but he's not and so, they think we're like them, but we're not. We are not products of short-term relationships. We know our dad. We grew up with him in our lives, stayed at his house; he introduced us to veggie dogs and coffee. He made us "skatemobiles" which were hand-crafted wooden scooters with a seat for your knee, and he painted them Rasta colors and let Nia and I ride them up and down his street until the streetlights came on. We met some of our half-siblings, but mainly we knew Edward, one of the oldest of the many we had. We knew his neighbors, the dirty little girls further down the street and the old couple that grew their own vegetables in the front yard. Our parents may have never married, but we still knew both of them.

As I get older, I will stop celebrating Father's Day. I watch my mom buy my sister dresses for multiple Father-Daughter dances she attends, tagging onto her friends' fathers while I sit at home, the idea of attending one of these dances never even crossing my mind. I decide that if I get married, I will walk down the aisle alone, not discussing the opportunity with my brother, cousins, or uncles.

Years will go by and I will blame myself for his death. My mom believes that I am depressed but won't tell me until she thinks I've fallen out of it. I will replay April 11th over and over, trying to see what was different about that day. Finally, I will pinpoint it to me saying "goodbye" instead of "I love you" when I left that day because I was excited for the Extravaganza. Thinking about it more, I will lose religion after I remember how my uncle prayed over my father in tongues only days before his death. I will blame God and myself for his death, for his absence, until I am fifteen years old. At fifteen, I will find myself in my first writing course writing about how I've blamed myself for seven years. But he was dying, I couldn't have fixed it.

I will meet people who don't know that my dad has died. Some will think that I'm lying and believe I'm just trying to cover up the gritty details of a relationship gone bad, of a father who left. It's not something I bring up in conversation; "Hi, I'm Negesti and my dad's dead," is not something I say. People find out when I'm ready to bring it up.

When I become obsessed with astrology, I will find out my dad was a Sagittarius, and my mom, a Pisces. Later, I will read somewhere on the internet that those two signs are the best fit parents for a Leo; I am a Leo. I will meet a Sagittarian boy and fall in love with him. On his own, he will find out that my dad died and believe that was my reason for cutting off my dreads. Besides this, he will know nothing about my dad, but on the ninth anniversary of his death he will be there for me as I silently walk the halls of my high school trying to hold it together. My best friend will tell him what day it is, chastising me because I didn't tell him, and he'll ask me if I need him, watching me from a distance for the rest of the day, just in case.

I find the sympathy cards that the kindergartners and third-grade students signed for Nia and me after it happened. I see my friends' names scrawled all over the card, over seventy-five signatures between the two of us and cards from four different classes. We missed close to a week of school when our dad died, and these were the apologies from our classmates for what had happened. The names are so messy, and I can't appreciate the card, thinking only that my eight- and nine-year-old classmates didn't understand, couldn't sympathize with me. I don't want an apology because there's no need to apologize for something that isn't their fault. Other people's sympathy seems fake, simple words said to make me feel better. But words won't bring him back, words won't turn back time, so that my mom actually listens when he complains of pain instead of brushing it off; I don't want anyone's words.

I have a hard time with emotions. It took me years to shed tears for the death of my father and actually feel that difference. I lack empathy, which makes people think I'm a cold person. How do I tell people that because I spent most of my childhood putting my emotions in a box—that was how I coped—I don't feel the way everyone else does. There was a long time between when my father died and when people I knew started losing people they loved. When my best friend tragically lost her uncle, I said what I knew: "That sucks." Because it does. It sucks. No one knows what you're feeling, no one understands what you've just lost, but they want you to feel better. What people don't realize is that in that moment, you don't want to feel anything at all.

In the decade or more since, I've learned that not every death needs a comment, not every death needs an apology. Sometimes, grief is best accompanied by presence and silence. I don't need to say what we already know: that it sucks, but I can offer space and comfort. As I watch people close to me begin to lose their parents, I feel like I have a role to play in their grief, as greeter to the Dead Parents Club. Welcome, I have been here for years, waiting, with my sister. I imagine we have pamphlets, tissues, fruit trays, casseroles—but none of it is enough.

Xavier was the first person my age that I met who lost a parent when they were young. His dad was killed when he was a newborn. I will find myself on the phone with Xavier late one night and he will ask me if I think it is better or worse having known my dad before he died. "I only knew him a little bit," I whisper.

"But you still knew him. I didn't know my dad." It's quiet on the line and I can tell he's thinking in the dark too.

"I'm glad I knew him, but I don't know which one's worse. I have someone to miss, and you don't have to miss anyone." I want to tell him that I have a void. An empty space inside of me that can't be filled, and I will try to fill it constantly and fail. Does he have that?

There are things I think about that make me feel guilty. I ate salami sandwiches at school even though I was supposed to be a vegetarian. And when my dad, a vegetarian, would ask me about my day, I'd lie and tell him I had a peanut butter and jelly for lunch. Once, I rested my hand on the cold metal barrel of a barely hidden shotgun under his bed and told no one I'd found it or touched it—and as a child, shouldn't I? It's too late to confess, now.

I pledged to myself that I will go to the house on Leonard Avenue before I leave the city for college, but I never made it. Anxiety and panic attacks as I get closer to the neighborhood or city will keep me from visiting. Seeing the sign on the highway for the exit twists my insides and the closer I get to his street, the harder it is to breathe and my vision tunnels as I clench my hands into a fist until I am far enough away. My dad was an artist, his house littered with paintings, drawings, and statues. At home, I walk past my father's hand-carved fisherman statue in the corner of the foyer and under the door chimes without noticing him, but he always seems to be watching us. The signed oil painting my dad painted will never be hung in the house, but always lean against a wall in the living room, collecting dust. Writing becomes my art because I am not a visual artist like my dad; so, I use words to paint pictures. I dedicated my first self-published book to him, but I got the death date wrong and it's too late to fix it and it makes me sick to my stomach.

My sister and I are the only daughters of both Edward Gaines and Helena Dameron. We don't have either of our parents' last names, but we have their blood. We are the only completely related siblings in both immediate families, but we have a stock of half-siblings on our father's side that faded from our life once the casket was lowered into the ground. I don't know how to spell any of their names, so I won't be able to find them. I look up my dad, trying to find out more about his family, vaguely remembering the stories of his parents, and after hours of searching, I find nothing on his Louisiana lineage.

My mom says I'm like him. My aunt says that I'm "just like Shaka" (my dad's nickname). I wouldn't know, but I bite down on the smile that wants to form. They mean I have his hoarding tendency, his selfishness, his sensitivity—all negative qualities, but they still say it with a glimmer of a nostalgic smile. My dad and I are both fire signs, both artists in our own way. I am twenty-seven years old. Today, my dad would have been eighty.

It was stomach cancer. That's what did it. That's what put him in the hospital where we visited for weeks before they sent him home with us and set up the makeshift hospital in our TV room. We watched television together and, in the days leading up to it, we watched old Extravaganza videos with him, sitting on the floor in front of the hospital bed. He was thin and getting thinner, the oxygen tube protruding from his nose and ruining my memory of his face. I slept in the adjacent room and every day before I went to school with my sister, I hovered over his bed in my MacEwen plaid jumper with my backpack on and kissed him on the cheek. And every day, until his last, I told him I loved him.

SELF-PORTRAIT FROM THE CORONER'S TABLE

Subject is a 25-year-old, Black female. Five foot and three inches. Two hundred and forty-four pounds. Eye color is brown. Hair color is naturally black, but subject has bleached her ends. On the anterior right side of neck there is one significant mole. Another one on posterior right of neck. A possible birthmark on anterior of abdomen, directly above belly button.

The Greek word *autopsia* translates to "to see for oneself." And when I approach the page, I am no longer just a writer, but I become anthropologist, psychologist, therapist, and critic all in one. An amateur at best, but a devoted one, seeking out answers through what I know best: form, lyric, language, and art. Essay as autopsy, as revelation, as resolution.

It's a form of punishment, writing too personally about myself. Something about my own body and personal experiences becomes too abject for me to digest and explore on the page in a vulnerable way. I end up using criticism, third-person, or fictive elements to try to discuss myself in an authentic way. There is too much trauma and anxiety taking up space in my body and it is too fuzzy here to look at myself without spiraling out of control.

How does one trigger herself?

There are only a few things that send me into panic: the most prominent things being death and the future—the latter being something my father didn't have, something that I'm trying to look forward to, but it's been almost twenty years without him, and with each year it seems more unfair. My father was older, sixty-two when he died, so I was never going to have the experiences so many fathers and daughters have—the clumsy primary school father-daughter dances, the cliché intimidation of prom dates, the breathless walk down the aisle—but still I grieve for the future we didn't have together, the alternate reality I'll never know. What does it mean if I can't help imagining all the what-ifs and could-have-beens?

Y-Incision.

I struggle to love my body because I believe no one else ever has, and I guess when you never have any validation that a single part of you may be right, you will only ever see yourself as wrong. In one way or another, I was always told I was wrong. Too big. Too hard. Not soft enough. Not weak enough. Too guarded. Too competitive. Too difficult. I can't remember if my lover actually ever loved this body or only the diamonds to be mined inside it. I can't remember if he ever took a second to take me in before taking me. Maybe I've forgotten all the positive things. I do that sometimes—the therapist called it a "negative feedback loop." *Think only happy thoughts*, she prescribed. Now I am an unabashed pessimist. I *do* remember the first time my mother called me pretty, how it was too late for me to believe it. And I think now she believes I'm pretty because I am beginning to look like her. I don't see it. I don't see anything good about myself.

It takes less to be broken than it does to build.

```
Removal of organs.
    Lungs.
    The subject's lungs have an ashy tint, which
confirms subject smoked tobacco short-term. Dam-
age is minimal, but noticeable.
```

I spent a few years clouding up hookah bars for hours at a time just to flirt with boys and girls and forget about my problems. And there's the secondhand smoke from all those times Mom picked up smoking when her iron was low and stress was high; from the smoke circulating through the air vents while my aunt chain-smoked menthols in her bedroom at night; and from my chain-smoking friends, who sometimes would politely ask, does this bother you? or change positions, so the smoke polluted the atmosphere instead of my face. And of course, all those blunts and joints I never realized had trace amounts of tobacco in them until years after developing a taste for flavored shells and papers.

```
Heart.
    The subject has layers and layers of scar
tissue around the left posterior of the heart.
Upon further examination, there is a 2 cm x 1.5
cm hole on the left ventricle. Subject would be
```

unsurprised, as she has spent her entire life trying to fill it with something else, but nothing lasts. Not even love. Note that as a child, subject imagined being buried with her heart in a vessel as is ancient Egyptian custom. Perhaps subject wanted to be prepared for judgment day and the weighing of one's heart against a feather. Subject is not an organ donor.

Maybe it's selfishness or possessiveness. Maybe it's young naiveté. Who needs a heart when they're dead? But the heart is one's entire essence, even with a hole. It adds character. Tell my ex-lovers that the hole is there, so maybe they can have a reason for why I could never be enough, maybe, in hindsight, they will learn what it means to compromise. Tell my mother that the hole has nothing to do with her, that it's been there for over a decade, and if I wasn't so avoidant of doctors, maybe someone would've caught it. The heart was never in the cards. First flip reveals: Seven of Pentacles. I thought maybe the hole was healing because I was feeling better, happier. I was finding new ways to care for others, to have and share love for them, to see them for their goodness and their flaws. I thought that if I could do all that for them, maybe I would be able to do that for myself.

Liver.
   Unremarkable.

Kidneys.
   Unremarkable.

```
Stomach and intestinal contents.

    Subject's stomach is stretched to the size
of a football, so much so, that one wonders if
it was ever actually the size of a fist. Inside,
there are remains of rice cakes and peanut butter
and pork chops and Brussels sprouts and rice and
zucchini and bananas.
```

Is it noticeable that I was counting the pounds? Stepping on the scale every other day to see if I would ever break 240# again? I don't know how to feel about my weight. It screams that I am not healthy, but everything else about my body argues that I am much healthier than my body type makes me look. Sometimes, I imagine what it looks like underneath my skin: hordes of fat tissue sitting atop muscle. Sometimes, I imagine cutting it all off me, the way I'd remove fat from a pot roast or chicken breast. There is just so much that it becomes overwhelming.

For a while, I didn't eat in front of men. Especially if I thought I'd be getting laid, I'd spend all day eating pretzels and drinking water or eating mangoes and drinking tea, so that this pussy would taste like nothing, so that this pussy would be perfect. After the orgasms or cancelled plans, I could finally eat a meal loaded with grease and sugar and caffeine and fat. That was when I cared. When I considered sex my vice. When I looked forward to being objectified by someone just because it meant not being alone. I don't believe in any of that anymore. Now all I do is eat in front of men, ignoring the filling falling from burrito onto the plate. Offering my food up to him and everyone else I'm with because I'm eating because I am hungry and I feel weird when they don't eat with me, when they watch me eat and play with their food. I eat because there's no real reason for me not to eat when I'm hungry, except that non-fat people don't like to watch fat people eat.

I can't imagine myself thin. I have never been thin. When I imagine the future, my body blurs.

```
Sample collection.
    Subject has two holes in both ears. The sec-
ond hole boasts small peridot stud earrings. Two
tattoos: one on right shoulder and another on
right thigh. Pockets hold the following items:
Trident Spearmint gum, Kroger receipt, MAC lip-
stick in DIVA shade, a single dollar bill and
dime; as well as one spearmint flavored Chap-
stick. Subject's hair was held up with a single
red hair tie and adorned with a black geometric
cotton headwrap. On her wrist, subject wore a
pink Fitbit activity tracker.
```

Leos are known for keeping souvenirs, and I began very early collecting small things from people who were once important to me. The items are hidden away in various storage containers at my mother's house, until one day, I tote them with me to my own home. I have an assortment of photographs, movie tickets, playbills, gifts, paperclip bracelets and rings, a rundown pair of drumsticks, and the most precious of all: handwritten notes, cards, and letters. I have nothing from the boy I fell in love with; we were supposed to always remain in each other's lives. Did he keep all the things I gave to him, including, but not limited to, my entire being? One day, it will be time for me to go through my keepsakes and begin throwing them away—some things are better left to fade in memory.

My father was an artist and a collector. He would take me and my sister to thrift stores, and we'd add to his collection. Sometimes, he took us to the junkyard where we would find lost remains of children's books and toys in the backseat of soon-to-be-demolished cars. I don't go to those places anymore. I've developed an aversion to used things—another deep buried trigger. Even books, I buy them all brand-new. But the collector gene is still strong: I constantly buy new notebooks, leaving half-filled ones to sit on the shelf or in boxes and containers for the day that I run out of things to write about and begin leafing through them, or maybe the day that I decide to write a poem again. I felt a lot of feelings when I was younger. I've trained myself to feel less and bury what I do.

```
Head and brain examination.
     Making primary incision—note that subject is
leaking letters slowly, now words are spilling
from the cranium as I continue making the inci-
sion. So many words and sentences and feelings
are careening onto the floor and soaking through
my soles. The subject had so much more to say,
she just didn't know how to articulate it.
```

Maybe this is the moment that the folds of my brain prove there was actually a much bigger issue at hand, a personality or mood disorder that I refused to find out was really there. But my mother always knew. She was always telling me to "get checked out" with a serious face that at the right angle morphed into a smirk.

Bipolar disorder and schizophrenia run in both my parents' families, but you can't claim it until it claims you, you know?

```
Conclusion.
    Closing up incision, making note that cause
of death is still uncertain.
```

I think sometimes, people like me for the things I represent or do, rather than for who I am. For instance, the seriousness with which I approach craft: endless ambition, self-destructive commitment and perfection-seeking. I can understand how these traits might be beautiful and make it seem that I love myself more than I actually do. I know that I love my family, my friends, and writing for the simple fact that none of these needs to be perfect to be authentic and honest. And one day I want to live honestly in the present, rather than in fear of the future and in fear of being placed into the role of sad girl, fat girl, Black girl, hard girl, lost girl, want-to-be-something-else girl.

There can be a life after purging everything and everyone that was truly wrong for you.

I didn't say it wouldn't hurt.

Leaning up on my elbows, I make the incision myself. I've watched enough *Grey's Anatomy* and dissected enough animals in lab to know how to pierce the skin deep enough without slicing through muscle. Pain is just your brain telling you to panic. Begin slow, bringing the blade down the sternum and pushing a little deeper to fold the flesh back. I reach my hand inside, feeling around with my fingers until I find it and squeeze the only reminder that I know how to survive.

RIPE

BEFORE I TURNED TWENTY-FIVE, I had graduated with a bachelor's and a master's, successfully
lived alone for an entire year, developed a writing
career, and amassed an outstanding amount of debt to do it
all. I had fallen in love several times, unsuccessfully. I had
lost my virginity without the flowers, fireworks, and high-fives
that teen dramas and romantic comedies had promised. I had
also destroyed, whether intentional or unintentional, most of
the relationships I'd entered my twenties with and replaced
some of them with healthier ones. I had lived in three different
states: one bitterly cold, one very mild, and the other a nice
temperate combination of both. Along with all of this, I had
also developed severe anxiety that on occasion spiraled into
high-functioning depression.

I always believed that twenty-five would be the magic number, the turning point of my life when everything would fall
into place in matters of love, money, and happiness. But now I
realize that I was conditioned to believe this because popular
culture makes it believable, especially having grown up in the
nineties and watching my favorite TV characters get their shit

together before they even graduated high school. In true form, they'd go on to meet and marry their college sweethearts, lose their virginities in hyper-romantic, painless scenarios, and eventually give birth to a perfectly happy and healthy baby about one to three years into that perfect marriage. Then, they'd bring that baby into their new home, and maybe struggle those first few months as homeowners and parents, but it was all worth it because by thirty, they'd have everything they ever wanted: home, family, and career.

I fell under the spell of twenty-five meaning I would be set up for a giant blessing to fall into my lap at any moment. In reality, my blessing was small and non-traditional, or rather, not what the dream sold me. I moved back into my mother's house with her and my aunt, sleeping in my sister's former bedroom with only the promise of a job as a part-time adjunct instructor at a local college.

In the few weeks before I actually turned twenty-five, I spent most of my time growing accustomed to my new adult life back at home: binge-watching *Law and Order: Special Victims Unit* for hours by day before falling asleep to the croon of *Steven Universe* at night. Sometimes, I would accompany my mother and aunts to lunch, or help entertain company over a game of Phase 10. But it seemed only heinous crimes and wholesome children's cartoons could help relieve the amount of stress I had about turning twenty-five and being single, without a home or apartment of my own or a high-powered full-time career to brag about.

When my mother was twenty-five, she was raising a four-year-old (my brother) and attending a local historically Black university to become a teacher. Eventually, she'd graduate at the top of her class. She lived in a predominantly Black city in southwest Ohio, renting a small apartment with enough space for the two of them. My aunt, when she was twenty-five, was married and raising and homeschooling five children in a home that she and her husband would eventually purchase. And my grandmother, at twenty-five, was already raising five children and pregnant with my mother. She was also married, living in a three-bedroom apartment in the first privately owned low-income housing development atop a rocky hill in eastern Ohio, along the border of Pennsylvania and West Virginia.

Growing up, adults made it seem like turning twenty-five and hitting that "quarter-life" checkpoint meant you were no longer a fledgling, but an adult ready to spread wings and survive on your own. When I was turning twenty-one, my coworkers were jealous of my excitement of birthdays, of my youth, warning me over drab salads and juice cleanses that "after twenty-five, birthdays aren't important anymore." Depending on when they started their careers, celebrities turned twenty-five surrounded by the gifts of their own personal success and independence. Kylie Jenner was already a (not self-made) billionaire. Forty-Five had inherited his father's real estate company and subsequent wealth. Jennifer Lawrence had an Oscar. Steve Jobs took Apple public. Beyoncé released *B'Day*. Adele was recording *25*.

There's an important common denominator between all those examples but one: whiteness. I'm sure there's a list somewhere on the internet chronicling the success of Black celebrities at twenty-five, but I couldn't find it. My point being that I personally didn't know any Black twenty-five-year-olds who were surviving completely on their own. But I did know many white twenty-five-year-olds who were married or in long-term relationships either roughing it alone in the world as a power couple or living comfortably in a suburban apartment, on their way to buying their first home or expanding their family. These days, having babies is less of a priority for most millennials when we know the planet is doomed. But I knew white people my age who were meeting those societal expectations of what twenty-five should look like. And I knew a few white people who weren't because of school or money or other circumstances. But I definitely didn't personally know any Black people who were meeting those same expectations. And when I asked, most of the Black people I knew at twenty-five were experiencing the same anxiety over nearing thirty and being single/jobless/poor that I was.

Legally, when you turn twenty-five, you can rent a car. That's really the only new thing you can do now, but if you went to a college with a Zipcar service, you might have already rented a car by then. At twenty-one, you could drink legally. But at eighteen—that all-foreboding age when the government decides you're an adult but your parents and professors (and maybe even a tiny piece of yourself) are all shrugging to themselves—you definitely don't know what you're doing. At eighteen, you could buy cigarettes, watch porn legally, create an online dating account, sign up for the military, or emancipate yourself from your guardian, if you wished. I turned eighteen and went to college, which was always part of my plan. I moved several states away to college, started inserting swears casually into conversations, and began chatting with men online as an inventive way to practice my sex-writing skills.

I remember the events of turning eighteen and twenty-one vividly. A Wiz Khalifa concert where I saw Amber Rose, even more stunning in person, smoke a cigarette above the pit as her then-boyfriend performed. And the first and last time I ever drank a Long Island iced tea—marked by six hours of vomiting and a wicked hangover that lasted four days. But when I turned twenty-five, I went to sleep on the couch because my uncle was in town for a family reunion. In the flurry of family events, my birthday existed on the periphery until I said it aloud: It's my birthday. My mother tried to make it an event: cake and a few gifts on a trip to the state fair. But the fanfare and celebration were awkwardly uprooted by the presence of extended family members I'd never met singing the "Happy Birthday" song, the volume of their voices dropping as they mumbled some semblance of my name.

Turning twenty-five made me sad, and it took years for me to finally shake that feeling.

I can tell you the exact moment when I believed I'd transitioned into adulthood. I was twenty-four. I had two jobs: one as a graduate student instructor and the other as a part-time editorial assistant. I was freelance writing and publishing work with moderate success. I'd cut ties with my last non-family roommate and decided I would move out and live on my own, knowing nothing about credit scores, leases, and how difficult it would be finding an affordable apartment in Chicago. For my third year of graduate school, I could have moved back home. But I refused to give up my two jobs, so I decided to (as my mother would say) "figure my shit out."

Running out of time and options, I paid a man $900 to find me an apartment cheaper than that. My $900 would replace my first month's rent. The apartment I settled on was owned by a racist landlord who called me a "good Black" during our first meeting, and the apartment was filled to the brim with the junk, medication, furniture, and more of a man who had "abandoned" it. Desperate, I looked past the hoard, past the squished carcass of a mouse on the back porch, past the Santa Marias posted up in the bathroom and living room, past the goldtone crucified Jesus hanging on the wall, past the poorly painted black walls, and saw the potential of the house once it was emptied, repainted, repaired, and filled with my belongings. Sue me for being an optimist.

The same day I moved in; the landlord had just started clearing out the house. Even my movers looked at me with concern as they hauled everything up the stoop and into the only empty room. It took a week for the house to be completely emptied of the previous tenant's belongings. It took another month for the black walls to be repainted beige. I ended up gathering a group of friends to finish painting the walls myself: a pastel blue for the bedroom and pastel green for the living room to soak in natural light. I bought a TV, a couch, a rug, and a bookshelf. I had the cable rerouted. I scrubbed and sprinkled the counters and floors with borax powder after seeing my first roach. I was prepared to befriend the first mouse, a chubby little Gus look-alike, but then one mouse turned to two mice and two mice evolved into me walking a half-mile away from the house every night in October with a live trap in a shoe box to go release them. And then the temperature dropped, and the heat had not been repaired by October 1st, the date when heat is legally supposed to be turned on by all landlords in Chicago. Mild fall weather morphed into a dangerous nine-degree temperatures one night. Another night, I set the mouse trap outside at 1 a.m. because I couldn't sleep listening to it squirm and squeak, trying to escape. It froze to death, falling from the trap onto the ground with a heavy thunk.

I was poor and paranoid, standing in my kitchen frozen in silence listening to the mice scramble from the upstairs apartment through the walls into mine. Eventually, I started staying on campus into the nighttime, afraid to go home to the apartment that I'd loved for its potential. I was a mess: laughing to my thesis advisor with bags under my eyes and telling him that I didn't have any pages and might end up moving out of state if I couldn't get my shit together. Two friends from graduate school helped me: a Gemini and a Virgo. They looked at my lease, they searched for apartments, and when I finally got approved to lease a new apartment in my dream neighborhood, they helped me pack up and leave and unpack and live. One of them drove me around the city, back and forth to Home Depot. The other lit sage and cleansed the deepest darkest corners of my new apartment after casually mentioning the two benevolent ghosts in my previous one. The night before I moved out, my gut told me to unplug the space heater that I'd been constantly running for the past few weeks to keep warm: The plug and socket had been melting into each other.

My new apartment was perfect, and it had heat. It was smaller than the one I'd abandoned but was free of vermin and the heat was on. It sat cozily on the lakeshore at the tippy top of the city, nuzzling Evanston, and I could ride the bus or train downtown to work on a consistent and dependable schedule. I lived across the street from one friend and four blocks down from another. I was within walkable distance of the beach, an Ethiopian café, a six-dollar movie theatre, Insomnia Cookies, and above whatever the Chicago-version of a bodega is for any of those late-night necessities. I was still a graduate student and working, but I was managing to hold myself above water in all aspects of my life: My relationships consisted of clear and honest communication, my work was exploring new territories, my new apartment was flooded with glorious sunlight throughout the day, my jobs weren't too strenuous or stressful, and I had some forgotten weed stashed away in my ottoman to celebrate all of these occasions. I'd entered 2018 with my head high, looking forward to my post-graduate future.

One of the things no one tells you about moving back to your hometown and living with your family is that you will regress to whatever age you were when you left. For me, I was eighteen. The house rules were: no boys, no booze, no drugs. At twenty-five, I still didn't have a license or drive. Moving back into my mother's house as an adult was especially hard because I didn't feel seen or valued as an adult except when it came to paying rent, buying my own groceries, and figuring out a way to make it to and from work (shout out to the COTA). Fortunately, I had learned and excelled at doing that in Chicago, where I had transitioned into adulthood in the most realistic, awkward way: with struggles and success and weight fluctuations. But though I was paying for everything I needed like an adult, I was treated as a child: spoken about in third person by relatives as if I wasn't in the room, chastised for dishes in the sink, chastised for an unruly room, and arguing with my mom about practicing driving her car, so I could finally get my license.

For the most part, I stayed in my room. On occasion, my mother and I would go to happy hour. And I would tolerate her though the second martini, which usually led to a tipsy confession or story about my father, a moment that could have meant something more sentimental, if it wasn't tainted with the aroma of vodka, lime juice, and blue cheese–stuffed olives. Many times, the second martini led to a fight or silence or to me wondering why my mother could behave like a nineteen-year-old and still demand respect, but I couldn't earn it at twenty-five.

During happy hour, I would watch my mother's mannerisms closely: the way she folded her hands on the table, how she sat poised straight instead of slouching, her silent gazes off into the distance; and the way she propped her chin on the palm of her hand, one elbow sitting on the table. I watched her because it didn't take long for me to notice that we mimicked each other: I would remove my chin from my knuckles, and she would prop hers up. W would take sips at the same time. We fluffed and folded our napkins simultaneously—in our silence, I would try to see myself in my mother, and I was there, but reserved: mirrored in her ethos. I had already departed from her twenty-something path; would I ever be able to converge and age as well as her—did I want to?

There are a lot of differences between now and the eighties, when my mother was navigating her twenties. We grew up different. She grew up in an age before parents became overpossessive of their children, when kids were allowed freedom to roam and mature and learn on their own. I grew up in two different eras: one of advancement and one of fear. Millennials had the fortune of growing up during the tech boom, when we rapidly escalated from no internet to 5G and Wi-Fi, from antennae cell phones to iPhones, from AM/FM to carrying any satellite radio station in our pockets. I've read that this rapid advancement has made millennials nostalgic for simpler days, which might translate to the anxiety that so many of us have been diagnosed with. Millennials are not Gen Z, which is to argue that there is some joy in our culture-based memories, there is an early period of time when we existed that wasn't controlled or weaponized by fear. But still, we went through puberty and transitioned into adulthood with fear. We were in our elementary school classrooms when the Twin Towers fell. We were exiting movie premieres to news of a massacre at the same midnight showing, hundreds of miles away. We saw New Orleans and her people get swept away by the current on national television. We became accustomed to stories of war and global tragedies. We were studying and sitting in lectures as other students were being gunned down during theirs. We sat in our dorm rooms and apartments, watching Black trauma manifest into a world aflame. Some of us recognized this fear and adapted to it. Others of us ignored it. All of us yearn for the past.

Biologically, I became an adult at twelve years old, blood spotting in my underwear. I was the last of my friends to bloom into a woman. Legally, I became an adult the summer of 2011, but I didn't buy a lottery ticket or a pack of cigarettes. Instead, I wandered into my favorite hookah bar, already an (underage) regular and chain-smoked several kohls' worth of white grape-flavored tobacco. I had grown up singing "We Don't Care" by Kanye West, rapping along to lyrics about surviving, never imagining that I wouldn't make it to twenty-five until the news started showing me bodies of Black children and young adults who didn't make it. Suddenly, every birthday included a moment of silence for the slain Black youth who didn't make it this far and a prayer for me simply being to see another bright August morning.

For Black girls who came of age in the nineties or early 2000s, when crop tops, miniskirts, lip gloss, hoop earrings, and Roc A Wear were the things to wear, chances are some-one—be it a creepy uncle, concerned cousin, strict parent, or favorite aunt—called her "grown" before she was even a teen-ager. Us Black girls were always destined to have a compli-cated adulthood, both biologically and socially. Our families and neighbors sexualized our bodies because of what we wore before we understood what sexuality was, and that played a big part in how we matured. For me, it was hoop earrings and lip gloss. For my sister, miniskirts. And maybe for you, it was a pair of platform booties or your first drugstore lipstick—but something in your head is associated with being "too grown" at a young age. We were chastised for or banned from wearing these things, so of course that first pair of hoops or designer lipstick feels different when you buy it in adulthood with your own money, feels different when you see if on carefree pre-teens or teenagers as an adult. When I see girls showing up to day camp with lips slathered in lip gloss, giving off enough sheen to blind me, I smile just slightly at their innocence and freedom. And then I wonder, who is telling them they're too grown instead of letting them be kids?

Socially, I became an adult when I moved to Chicago for grad-uate school because for the first time, I had to figure every-thing out on my own. If there was an emergency, no one could show up in less than six hours. Did I call my mom when I saw the first mouse? I did. And she told me to either move or get a cat. Did I cry outside of the three-story Walgreens on Fullerton when I got my first ear infection in Chicago? Of course, I had been there for only a week and antibiotic ear drops range from $80 to hundreds. Did I think about moving back home, to the safety and familiarity of my family? Every single day for an entire year, trying to convince myself that I hadn't made a mistake in picking up and moving away from everything and everyone I knew for the second time in my life. No one tells you that adulthood means spending every single day wondering if this long-awaited independence was a mistake.

My age, my genetics, my Blackness, my gender, my trauma—I was destined for worry. In college, I spent most of my time wondering if schizophrenia was going to become part of my future, part of my identity. Its impact hovering on both sides of my family tree. Every time I plunged into a depressive episode or found myself frozen with anxiety spiraling into dread, I was reminded of what loomed in my blood and brain. Twenty-five was the estimated end of my watch period, at the end of which I would know if this incredible amount of stress, worry, and dread would transform into or trigger a complete break from reality. What would it look like and how would it feel? I imagined a light switch in a far-off area of my brain collecting dust from being off for so long—what world and reality would be revealed if it ever clicked on?

I had a goal of bring twenty-five with a house, husband, and full-time career, and not enough people told me that it was unrealistic. I graduated with immense debt and struggled to find a full-time job that offered healthcare benefits and a salary. As I write this, I still don't have a salary. But at least now I have healthcare. I imagined I would graduate and become a full-time professor, but that didn't happen. I somehow managed to find a job in higher education, doing something I love and believe in. I learned how to morph my two English degrees into supplemental income by freelance writing and editing. When that wasn't enough for a decent livelihood, I started substituting at the same K-12 school that helped prepare me for this chaotic adult world. Eventually, I wrote the perfect cover letter and was charming enough in an interview to be offered my first full-time, adult job—six months into my quarter-life crisis.

I shouldn't call it a crisis. I had a roof over my head, water to bathe and brush my teeth, food to eat, and even on occasion alcohol to drink. But socially and emotionally? So many of my friends were trying to make the most of their twenties by traveling, dating, and partying as I took their phone calls hiding away in my bedroom between episodes of *Law and Order*. I was a wreck, emotionally, rarely fighting with my mother but when sparks flew, they escalated into slammed doors and tears, with me panicking about having nowhere else to go. My only escape from stress became the gym, so I started training to get stronger. I relished the half hour a day when I could stop thinking and just sweat, struggle to breathe, and exhaust myself to feel good. I had only one goal, which was to survive.

I laughed each time one of my friends entered the twenty-five threshold with similar stress and panic. I replay a quote in my head by Tina Knowles: "If you're going through it, just know you're going through it. You're not going to get stuck there, you're going to survive." And I did, practically unscathed: with fewer friends, transient high blood pressure, severe anxiety, and a perverse sense of optimism that only appears in times of crises and panic. Somehow it works out. But it's nothing like the dream we were sold, which seems to always be the case. Gen Z makes fun of millennials because we always complain about the horrors of adulting. What else can we do but complain? Especially for those of us whose parents aren't coddling us, those of us with bills to pay, people to take care of, and responsibilities to follow through on. There isn't really a choice. Fly or flounder. Eat or be eaten. When my mom was twenty-five, the average rent was $225 a month and minimum wage was $3.35, which is equal to $7.82 with inflation. When I lived alone in Chicago, thirty years later, rent for my one-bedroom apartment was $950 a month, but minimum wage was $7.25. It feels as if this country set millennials up for failure, the same way it did women and Black people.

The difference between maturation and evolution is that the latter typically only gets better, more advanced; whereas the former implies that eventually one rots and dies. One is linear and the other is a cycle. The ones who set us up for failure are getting older and older, resisting change in the world while the rest of us try to adapt. Sometimes these older men appear on social media, randomly requesting to follow me, with their misspelled and grammatically incorrect bios. They are looking for sugar babies, for young women who are looking for cold, hard cash and willing to chat, date, and photograph to get it. I could be one of those women. I think about these Boomer sugar daddies often: Not all wealth is inherited, but we've all got bills and I make an entertaining date.

The truth is, I didn't know what it meant to be grown or an adult when I was twenty-five, and even still, I find myself changing and adapting daily. From my perspective, the year I turned twenty-five tried to destroy me. Others might have considered it a coming-of-age test. What I've learned is that adulthood will never meet any of our expectations. I write this retrospectively, at twenty-six, twenty-seven, and beyond, navigating spaces I could have never planned for: a global pandemic, wearing masks at a coffee shop, an era of civil unrest only comparable to that of the 1960s—what semblance of pop culture was supposed to prepare me for this?

The trick about picking mangoes is figuring out when they are ready to be eaten. I once cracked a filling by biting into an unripe mango, which led to a root canal at twenty-four. And I've waited too long to slice open the fruit, revealing a sticky, pulpy mess of yellow falling away from its rind. I want to offer you tips on how to expertly pick a mango from the bin at the grocery store. I want to give you the same anecdote someone once told me: The best mango is the one you walk outside and pick from the tree. But the likelihood of you and I picking a mango from a tree while the sun rises slowly from the east and the only noise punctuating dewy silence is that of bugs and birds rising to greet it? It's low. I can only tell you what I did and still do. I prefer the mangoes grocery stores import from Mexico: They are a medley of green, red, and yellow, and larger than other mangoes. I start with a gentle squeeze, and if the rind budges too much then the fruit is ripe and will be no good by the time it gets to my kitchen counter. If it doesn't budge at all, it's too firm and means that I will have to play a dangerous waiting game at home on deciding whether it's ready to cut open or not. It's a calculated test: not leaving an impression of your fingers on the fruit while at the grocery store. Smelling the base of the stem. It's similar to old wives' tales about smelling the base of a pineapple to see if it's sweet, slapping watermelons to hear specific timbre of ripeness, or planting tomatoes with a sprinkle of sugar to make them sweeter. If the stem smells sweet and has a little bit of sap around it, then that's the mango I choose.

All this is to say that I work very hard to make sure I've selected the perfect mango and could still end up letting it over-ripen on my kitchen counter or cutting into it while its insides are still a pale yellow and not the infamous Indian yellow one might find glistening in an oil painting by Vermeer. Adulthood is the same. I find myself in spaces constantly surprised by what is happening before me. Even the year 2020 revealed itself to be one giant contradiction: I began it with my best friend and sister and I, high off a single mulberry gummy edible, toasting champagne glasses into the air as balloons floated to the floor around us. I have video of myself going to toast the camera—you know, one of those cute videos you take to post later on Instagram—and I spill my drink on the way down to my lips. And I thought, this is how the year will be.

Each New Year for the past decade, my sister and I have come home from a night out with our best friend, sporting furs and high heels, and we pause in the driveway to make sure there is at least a dollar in our pockets, another old wives' tale our mother reminds us of annually. Then we trek in, making our way to the shower to scrub off the previous year. But in 2020, three months after our New Year's toast, I was sent to work from home indefinitely. Four months later, the governor had shut down the state and the only places to go outside of the house were the grocery store, pharmacy, and gas station. Six months into the year, the city was placed on curfew—and as the sun went down, my friends and I sat sweating in the doorway of an apartment listening to *The Life of Pablo* by

Kanye West, sipping on take-out margaritas and remembering the simpler summers of 2011 and 2016. At exactly 10 o'clock, around the corner from our house, Dairy Queen shut off its lights, served its last patrons, and the streets weaving away from downtown Columbus went quiet.

After I moved home, it took an entire year for me to adjust before I was ready to hang out with people my age and socialize again. And even then, I was hesitant about navigating the city I loved and running into people I knew who might have expected more from twenty-five-year-old me. I was single and living at home with my mom and aunt. I was gearing up for teaching part-time at a local arts college. A few years later, I am still single, working two jobs, and living at home with my mom and sister. I still teach at the arts college, putting my very expensive degree to good use. In the winter, I create art and pitch freelance work because it's too cold to do anything else. When I'm not in the mood for artmaking, I cook, often and a lot, because making food is the closest I can get to writing an essay. This version of me, she takes Prozac daily to quell the dread that slinks into any silence she comes face-to-face with. She spends her hard-earned money on therapy. She spends a lot of the time dreaming about the things she expected to have at twenty-five, only to learn that there is no treasure map to them. She can't just *find* X and be happy.

I used to believe one of my most toxic traits was living in the past because I was afraid of the future. I spent a lot of time analyzing and revisiting the moments that I believed helped me become the woman I am today, but really those memories were just a comfortable place to exist. Much more comfortable than waking up and not knowing what the day would look like. The present is strange and full of worry some days. Whether a surreal presidency or an ongoing pandemic, there's not much I can do about the future besides fret and panic. So, I'm trying to do what people who have learned to manage their thoughts do: take it one day at a time. Often, it's frustrating. Rarely is it boring, but one thing I've learned— possibly exacerbated from living through a pandemic—is that time moves fast. Days move slow, but the world still spins as expected. Adulthood has welcomed me with open arms whether I wanted it to or not. For a long time after my dad died, I could only imagine a future version of me as a blur. Even now, I can't see how my life will look in five years, but I've spent a long time making sure that I won't be a blur.

CONTEMPLATING GOD

UNLIKE MY COUSINS, who grew up in the church, I was not brought up religiously. My family did not go to church. We celebrated Christmas by gathering to eat ham and greens as a family. In my household, there was a god and sometimes we referred to that god as God and sometimes as Jah. At one time, both my parents were Rastafarians—another Abrahamic religion—believing in Jah and Afrocentrism, revering Ethiopia and her symbol: the lion of Judah. But God was a man and you believed in him, or you didn't, no one really cared. For me, God was a man, and everything that happened was supposed to happen. Then my father died. And when I asked for signs, for answers, when I prayed, craving some sort of omniscient response—my god didn't answer. I stopped believing. My mother and sister sought the church; I found the page.

•

An ex-lover speaks Her into existence: *Black female God.* Isn't a female god a goddess? Play with the words: God as a female, not a goddess. Not just a female, but a Black one. Ex-lover wants to trifle with the patriarchy. And I think of those t-shirts that people wear: "I'VE MET GOD AND SHE'S BLACK." How easy—how natural—it is to pair God with He/Him/His because the people writing about God were men and they proposed that man had a son and man crafted man and man was crafted into woman. But where was She?

It seems like women are always associated with the earth. Our goddesses are Mother Earth or agriculture-related or women-related. They are supple-breasted, curvaceous women, with hair flowing down their backs or elegantly braided and crowned. They are affiliated with elements and locations, beauty and fertility, family and romance. Very rarely do we see goddesses of war or death. Where are the goddesses with grit—the commanders of chaos? These women goddesses are scattered across religions, but there are not enough. If the earth is a product of a woman's birth, then women must be magic—but also tended to, taken care of, and harvested.

I remember the first time someone truly listened to what I had to say: my first writing class in ninth grade. Our assignment was to interrogate a pomegranate: feel it, touch it, smell it—we passed it around the table. And my teacher supplied us with a random bit of information: Most likely Eve plucked a pomegranate from the tree—a Judaic theory for a fruit that permeates the barrier of religion. I began to feel an affinity for Eve, considering what I'd have done in her situation. I had already strayed from religion, leaning more towards knowledge, to the concrete. The fruit was offered to me, and like Eve, I ate the seeds. In her classroom, I bloomed. I opened up on the page, allowed myself to be vulnerable. I wrote about my father, how I blamed myself for his death, how I'd spent the previous eight years living with that silent burden. And people were listening to my work, asking me to read it aloud and share with them my secrets. I began honing a power: feminine and raw, a hungry flame.

My ex-lover is trying to bridge biology and religion by making God a Black woman. His argument is birth. His argument converges both evolution and creationism, saying that She must have created evolution in order to create man, that she birthed the universe. I imagine a Black woman made up of stars, her legs wide open, and out falls the Milky Way, a string of creamy white. Then Venus, Jupiter, Mars, Saturn, Uranus, Neptune, Mercury, and after a long pause—the silence stretching in a space that has no concept of sound—Earth. It only seems right that She carved out a piece of her own soul to mold into Sun, allowing it to illuminate her newly born planets floating in disarray.

We're both writers, but he believes he should have been a philosopher. I ask if that's because he wants to ask questions without having answers. He says something vague about questioning life and rejecting society, to which I can only roll my eyes and wonder: Maybe he should have been a philosopher. But instead, he's a writer and the only thing he can do with his questions is write them down and play with sound and hope that the cover of his book is interesting enough that someone will want to read his questions and ponderings. I ignore him, more intrigued with Black female God. I want to know Her. I want to feel Her. I want to believe that somehow my essence embodies Her. Black female God. He thinks about it from the perspective of a man: Who gave birth to Adam?

But instead, I imagine an exhausted Black female God, floating in the universe surrounded by her planets, the waxiness of afterbirth causing them to orbit around her. The original homebirth. And maybe She inspects each planet before choosing Earth from the middle of the litter. She trails her fingers across its fragile surface, accidentally creating crevices and surface flaws, continent and ocean.

He states: *Nothing just exists.* Except for Black female God. Where did She come from? Is she an orphan? Does she have siblings in other galaxies? Is she not a god, but rather a titan? Is she made up of stars, and thus, like us, a being of quivering molecules? In fits of rage, does she implode? A supernova. Or worse, the collapse of the sun. Is that how the world ends?

He pulls me into his thinking, and I am transported back to a time before I stopped loving him and before I began. We sat in the back of the library, hidden behind the shelves, innocently leafing through mythology books. I wanted to be Apollo or Aphrodite, my fingers trailed over the illustration of her blooming from a shell, draped in loose cloths.

He asks me, *Are you a virgin?* And suddenly, I was Artemis, sole protector of the forest, virgins, and children.

Is Black female God a virgin? The way Adam and Eve were meant to remain? Her hymen stretching before snapping back into place after producing the planets. Can She take two fingers, reach deep inside herself, and scoop out stars? After all, She is God. Impenetrable.

If God is a Black woman and She created the planets, where would Adam and Eve fit in? Eventually, she had to create life. Black woman God, eclipsing the light as she spun Earth around on the pad of her finger, wondering what was missing. A dark planet reflecting her own skin in its land, her eyes in its water. For the first time, She sees herself. And it is a birth, rather than a creation, as she gathers dust from the universe, weaving them together with breath, maybe whispering an incantation for life or strength before dropping it into the dark, listening for the splash.

And She waited.

When I told him I prayed for him, he told me he knew. Is that how prayer works? Is it like that idea of when someone is dreaming about you, you can't fall asleep because you're awake in their dream? Were my prayers for his strength and well-being instant-messaged to his soul? I can't remember if he said he prays for me. And even if he did, I wonder what he's praying for, what is it that he thinks I need, what is it that he thinks I'm missing? Isn't that what prayer is for—to send something to someone, be it love, hope, faith, or strength? A prayer can be anything: a song, a word, a name, a mantra. There are the prayers my elementary school forced us to recite before lunch, the ones my mother says aloud before family dinners, my sister's silent ones at every meal, the dipping of fingers into holy water at silent mass, a simple hug or a hand squeeze. I don't know if anyone is praying for me—should I feel it?

I had created a parallel: Love felt like God and prayer felt like love. I'm not sure I've ever had both at once. I found a warm comfort in the idea that someone cared about me, even if that someone was omniscient and only a potential. At night, in the dark, staring at the ceiling or with my eyes squeezed shut, I spoke to God about the things I couldn't control. I prayed for my family, best friends, my no-longer friends, and even for my current and former lovers. Everything melted away: fear, worry, loneliness. I wonder if my prayers reach God's ears as a whisper, a single whisper in a chorus of millions—or if She were there, in the stars, in the crisp air, sitting cross-legged with her head tilted, my prayer floating into her omnipresence, squeezing through her pores. Does She sit at the foot of my bed and write everything down? I desperately want someone to be listening.

It's not like using the potter's wheel. She is creating life, and so, she must be patient. How many attempts did it take God to be successful; did she peek at her creation on Earth, concealing herself in the water, in the clouds? Or did she try to entertain herself with other things: new planets, new galaxies, drawing constellations in a distracted manner? Black woman God births the earth and must wait to see the results.

We should stop thinking the existence of man is an "either/or" and start considering "and": creationism *and* evolution. Is it ego that makes us want to be the reason for this planet's existence? Why does the ego need to rule so desperately? My high school biology textbook had a fish with legs on the cover, that was it. It was my formal introduction to the subject of evolution, something my family never discussed. In college, I took another biology class on evolution, but this time I was mapping skeletons and bodies of vertebrates through time. Even as I sat in biology classes, throwing my hand up with a fierce consistency, I knew that there must be a way that everyone was right. It's possible the story of humans has been misreported, misremembered, mythologized by the men who recorded it. But I also knew that a fish walking out of the water one day to find more resources made more sense than my exponentially great-grandmother being carved from the rib of the first man.

I believe in evolution because of bones. Invertebrate to vertebrate. Jawless to jaws. The same jaw bones in an alligator, evolving, shifting upwards for the bipedal into ear bones. I've laid out the skeletons in front of me, studied the shape and function of bones. And maybe She pieced together Eve with the structures that she liked: a schematic for humanity based on the animals who came before.

Why would we not be created as equals? A ploy for men to constantly put women in their place: *Remember, that's my rib you're using; see the sacrifices I've made for you?* I reject this. I want to expertly slice open my abdomen with a scalpel, reach in, and break off my floating ribs with a bare hand. I want to give Adam back his gift.

Black woman God did not intend for a hierarchy. She makes Eve first, molding clay into her own image. Or it's possible, she tinkered with Her first creation and watched it evolve. But woman came first. Woman came first and somehow gave birth to man.

He says, *If the serpent was male, how did woman become the first to sin? Wouldn't man be the tempter?* But angels are not men. He brings up Lucifer, and I imagine the angel cascading to the surface of the earth like a meteor: ablaze, his wings burning to a crisp as they fall off from the velocity. Maybe that's where man came from. I used to sympathize with the devil because of my own pride, because of my desperate need to be recognized, because of my own need for power. My need for validation morphed into an ego built on insecurity—if no one loved me, I'd need to do it myself; if no one listened, I'd need to force them to hear.

If God is a Black woman, would she have granted Lucifer his own domain, would there even be a hell? What does it mean if Lucifer is a Black angel, a Black man? Or would She have picked him up between her forefinger and thumb, crushing him into dust before scattering his remains across her galaxy? I doubt she would stand for his drama. Hell would have been created from something inside of her, something dark. Perhaps hell comes after humans have forgotten Her, after ego has replaced the supernatural. And maybe hell is shadow woven together, so its inhabitants end up lost in the thick of it.

He thinks God is a Black woman. Which I think is ironic considering how he's treated women: the façade of a Black man searching for his queen. Black queen meets Black man, and Black man feels safe, secure. Black man is insatiable for love and validation. Black man looks for something with a different taste, spicier, alluring. I have been that different taste, been that something that Black men love to sample, but never want to have. He was one of them. I don't tell him any of this but remain silent as he convinces himself that God is a Black woman. If this is the case, then why hasn't She taken her thumb and crushed man back into bone, back into soil?

Sometimes I feel like I'm missing something. I believe my father's death bored a hole in me that is clean around the edges and unfillable. And since I struggled to forgive God for taking him away, it remained empty. I tried to fill it with flirting, with schoolwork, theater, words. Eventually, I tried to fill it with sex, which might have made the hole bigger, made the edges messier. Because the men I loved used me to fill their own emptiness, and I did for a time. For a while, I even tried to fill my void with smoke, but eventually that disappears too.

I want God to be a Black woman, but I see Her bent over and breaking, sweat crystallizing on her forehead. Her hair wrapped up in a galactic scarf as she carries the earth, swaddled on her back, colicky and warm. She has to check on the other planets, her universe, and create more stars. She wipes her brow, watching the crystals fall into the galaxy, hardening into charcoal-gray asteroids. Sometimes she mistakes her sweat for tears or her tears for sweat and watches in silence as they fall and float in front of her, reminding her of what she's created.

No one respects a Black woman. Except for other Black women. I don't look in the mirror, believing that I am a replica of God, that God is a She. But if She is alone, then she must be a Black woman: lording over her universe, birthing the planets, and blooming life by pulling from her own body. We are always pulling from ourselves, always giving ourselves away. A curly follicle of hair might be stretched into the trunk of a tree; tears and sweat may have salted the ocean; sloughed-off skin cells may have been heaped to create the soil. There's no one to disrespect her if She's alone.

I think of how it seems that Black women are less than everything. And yet, I spend much of my time stressing over who will stand up for the Black men because I know no one will stand up for the women. I am hesitant to believe in the Black man who wants the same for Black women that he does for himself. When will our subconscious European patriarchal standard kick in? When does the Black man begin to consider himself more like the white man than his mother? And yet, I feel obligated to stand up for the men, to defend them from the world. I position myself as guardian of men without expecting reciprocity. I constantly consider my potential husband and son. How I will take care of him before he considers me as more than a body. How I will become nurturer, teacher, pleasurer, and protector. What I must ask myself: Am I willing to die for him, even if he wouldn't do the same?

Meanwhile, Black women are missing and dying all over the country. We are murdered by strangers, the police, husbands, boyfriends. We are dying during labor at an alarming rate. Our bodies are pillaged without consequence. We are silenced and invalidated by our white audiences and peers. Black women are literally disappearing at alarming rates, like the honeybees, and instead of working to prevent our extinction, the world contemplates an artificial solution as the remedy.

He tells me not to worry about the men. *Our egos will support us*, he says. Which is typical of a man, to reject protection from a woman, to feed into the primitive way of things: man as provider, woman simply provided for. But woman provides the men, does she not? They stretch and contort her body in ways she couldn't prepare for—creating a pain that will never be forgotten, will never be apologized for, will always be forgiven.

He told me once—we were listening to "Grenade" by Bruno Mars—that he would "catch a grenade for me" and that was probably one of his ways of saying that he loved me. That night, we slow-danced in a parking lot as it rained. I told him I wouldn't jump in front of a train for him.

Another time, he told me that I had to die first because I couldn't live without him. I wanted to tell him he was wrong, that I could make it on my own because I was the only one who'd ever stood up for myself. I was the only one who'd ever fought my battles. I was both defense and offense.

Is this how Black woman God feels? Is there a specific type of arrogance that comes with being God or is She humble and devoted to serving her creations, providing for them without reciprocation? A few curls escape from the tight bun of hair sitting atop Her head as she makes sure we have everything we need, that we can survive. She waves the curls out of the way and convinces herself that we still love her, even if the prayers are dwindling.

What is the purpose of this privileged existence? Why couldn't we just be made up of stars too?

Of course, it's possible that my God is androgynous. When I was younger, I took online personality quizzes about the percentage of male and female I was and always ended up with 50 percent of each. And I'm sure that has nothing to do with my above-normal levels of testosterone and my own estrogen-related struggles. I think I care too much about men. I've spent years working to understand them, picking at their brains. And from what I've learned and experienced, I probably shouldn't care. Promises have been broken, my body has been used, I've been forgotten. But I desperately long to protect the Black men, constantly thinking about their livelihood.

Androgynous Black God—what do they look like?

He asks me: *But what if God split into man and woman?*

I ask him what the difference would be. But I can imagine two Black bodies: one male, one female, standing beside each other before welding into one intersex supernatural being. They run a hand through the short curls on top of their head before twisting a single curl in the back with a finger. We make eye contact, and I feel myself shrinking.

My prayers are now a stream of whispered thank yous and an overwhelming feeling of unworthiness. It's very hard for me to acknowledge my accomplishments—one of the things I developed from years of loving a man who didn't love me back, of burying myself in work without validation. And then I moved to Chicago, where I was alone. I had to recognize Chicago and my writing talents as blessings—as positive consequences of years of depression being spun into essays, a ruthless work ethic from constant self-deprecation—and that, for once, I was where I was supposed to be at that exact moment in time: fate. So, I ask for very little from Them, only that everything goes according to plan, and They'll provide me with whatever I need to succeed and continue on the right path. But I still wonder who I'm speaking to.

I don't know where he and I stand, but I still feel that intellectual and natural pull to him that makes me wonder if he still thinks of me. On occasion, I find myself lost in thought and his silhouette appears in my periphery, but I don't reach out. I'm afraid we've reached an impasse, and contrary to what I expected, I've left him. I couldn't grow with him.

Once, I had a dream—nightmare—that he was dead, and I was locked in a soundproof glass room because I couldn't stop screaming. I flooded the room with tears. I woke up to my throat feeling raw.

There was a part of me so desperate to worship and be worshipped, that if he'd loved me wholly, I would have let him be God.

But I was also desperate to implode.

I hear androgynous Black God in music. I have no doubt that it's Their voice that consumes the artist and crawls into my ears, bringing me back to Them, back to God. They choose their words carefully and pour in the emotion, similar to Aquarius: an ankle-length weave crumpling at their feet as They kneel with the vase, voice streaming into it like water. Their music is the patter of the rain, the lull of cascading waves. Omniscient, They coat the artist's trachea, coaxing the air upward, forcing sound to burst through lips.

This is not a prayer. But the page lends itself to me as a space for worship, a space to ask questions. And there are few witnesses to my renewal and growth, but the most consistent has been the essay. An archive of me trying to rebuild that relationship with Her or Them, with myself. I've lost many friends along the way, and they still laugh at me and proclaim that I'm an atheist or I don't believe in God. They don't know me anymore. But do they know my God?

If God is a Black woman, then She is Atlas. And to this theory, he never responds. In the original myth, Atlas separates Earth from the heavens, standing on the western edge, spine curving into permanence under the weight of the universe, the weight of gods and goddesses.

There is God: thick, brown and black dreadlocks falling in front of Her face, star-filled veins bulging under dark skin as she uses all her strength to hold up her home away from us humans. What did we do to revoke the privilege of frolicking with God?

RECLAIMING A NAME

I'M LISTENING TO "I" BY KENDRICK LAMAR for the first time, on his sophomore album *To Pimp a Butterfly*. And the difference between "i" on the album, and the single, is that the album version is a live recording of Lamar performing the song, during which he stops in the middle to educate the audience on the status of Black people in 2015 as a people under attack. I'm concentrated on his speech about the country, his culture—my culture, our culture—when he spits:

> *Well, this is my explanation straight from Ethiopia*
> *N-E-G-U-S definition: royalty; king, royalty—wait,*
>   *listen*
> *N-E-G-U-S description: black emperor, king, ruler,*
>   *now let me finish*

I pause the song. That's my name. I rewind it, wondering why no one told me that Kendrick Lamar was rapping about my name, wondering if anyone got excited to hear the roots of my name being explained as a motive to overcome oppression and reclaim a word and a world that refuses to let us be.

Of course, no one did. Because no one knows that's the root of my name, because how do you get Queen (Nigiste Negestatt) from King (Negusa Nagast), how does man become woman without the loss of a rib and a sacrifice of power? But Lamar has revealed a Black inheritance in an era when young Black women had started calling each other "Queen" and Black men "Kings," and Black hair was once again being celebrated in its natural state. The word "Negus" began appearing next to people's names on Twitter and in their Instagram bios with crown and brown fist emojis. Kendrick Lamar inspired that, a kid from Compton—that's power.

To Lamar, "Negus" is a homophone for "niggas." Breaking it down phonetically as /nigūs/ or "nih-gus," and he raps: *The homies don't recognize we been using it wrong*, proclaiming a second reclamation of the word "nigger." A consistent progression from "nigger" to "nigga" to "Negus," so we can rightfully assume a throne crafted by ancestral Black hands, by African hands. I applaud Lamar for his producing a cultural self-love anthem with "i," for *To Pimp a Butterfly* existing as a Black empowerment album, but I do have my reservations. Like what about the time a white boy and his friend giggled before confessing to me that my name sounded like "nigger" and that was how they remembered how to pronounce it wrong, getting the first syllable and the hard *g* right, but the second and third syllables wrong. What to do about the time that someone associated my name with a slur, my royal name, with its century-old Ethiopian roots? And I don't mean like Becky. Because Becky is easy to pronounce and conjures up an image of a smiling white face, because no one laughs, stutters, or pauses before calling Becky's name during roll call.

My name, so rooted in Blackness that people are always disappointed to find out that I am not from Ethiopia or anywhere in Africa, but simply a Black girl from Ohio, whose parents were born in the United States. A Black girl who can't trace her roots because of a surname.

Which name is the white surname adopted from the slave owner, the name that migrated its way through generations? Which name belonged to him? Which name was modified to taste like freedom? Is it Gaines from my father or Dameron from my mother? It could be neither. My name is neither. I want to know where I am from, to understand my roots, to map my way across the diaspora, to know the name carved onto the side of the boat that carried my ancestors, shackled and crowded like livestock, across the Atlantic.

I'm lost, missing. They ask me where I'm from and roll their eyes. They ask me where my parents are from, which parent is Ethiopian. They ask me where my name comes from—not meaning its origin or etymology, but how did I, a Black girl, get an African name if I am not African?

In a patriarchy, you get your name from your father. The United States is built on patriarchy and grafted of European traditions. In the United States, names are important. Names are how one cements a place for oneself. Names are recognition, status.

How do you destroy a person's humanity? Strip him of his name.

How do you reclaim your humanity? Choose or create a name.

How do you own another person? Give her your name.

The barista at the local Starbucks calls me "Roxy," because I offered my middle name as the name to put on the cup. Sometimes people burst into renditions of songs that have the name "Roxanne" in them. At the club, men hitting on my friends will nod at my name and politely smile. I don't enjoy telling random strangers my name, slowly repeating its proper pronunciation as they lean in closer, their ears near my mouth. They will repeat it incorrectly, and I shrug. Chances are, I will never see this human again in my life. Sometimes, they will ask me to repeat my name over and over until they finally get it. If they repeat it correctly, I am taken aback, shocked that they didn't say it wrong.

When I went to college, my sister asked me if I would tell people how to say my name correctly.

For years, I'd pronounced my own name wrong because it was easier, it fit into other people's mouths better.

My mom wants me to embody my name. "I gave you a strong name," she says.

There was only one woman crowned in Ethiopia's monarchy: Zewditu. In 1917, Zewditu became the first and only empress of Ethiopia. They created her title from the king's, and she was the "Queen of Kings." She was never actually allowed to rule on her own during her thirteen-year reign, instead forced to have her male cousin (and later her successor) around to exercise her power. Zewditu wanted to preserve the Ethiopia that was, rather than work to build the modern Ethiopia that could be. She folded into her values and religion, allowing her cousin to be in charge of the political decisions. The church loved their queen, and the queen loved her god, all the way to the end—

Does the name make the person strong or vice versa?

I am not the queen of anyone. I rule only over my own domain. I do not own a crown or have many expensive things. But I believe I am stronger than many expect me to be, and I know my mother is proud. So, when you pronounce my name, imagine that all the *E*'s are *I*'s. The *G* is hard. You've almost got it. Perfect.

NOTES

Versions of the following essays in this collection were previously published or exhibited. A big thank you to the editors, readers, and contest judges of each publication for taking the time to consider and house my work.

"Reclaiming a Name" was published online for The Normal School (2021).

"Contemplating God" was a finalist in the nonfiction prize contest for *Phoebe Journal* (2020).

Images and text from "For Your Pleasure" were excerpted and published in *Best American Experimental Writing 2020*.

"Marginalia" originally appeared in *Fourth Genre* vol. 23, no. 1, 2021, pp. 17–28, and was a finalist in the nonfiction writing contests for *Gulf Coast* (2020), *Fourth Genre* (2020), and *Black Warrior Review* (2018).

"The One Where My Femme Swallows You Whole" was published in *Storm Cellar* vol. 9, no. 1, and was the winner of *Storm Cellar*'s Force Majeure Flash Contest (2020).

"Messy: Brief Notes on Body Positivity" was published online for *Wear Your Voice* magazine in their Body Positivity series (2019).

"Nine Minutes" was published online for *IDK Magazine* issue no. 5 (2019).

"Perspectives no. 4.1" and "Perspectives 4.2" from *For Your Pleasure* were published for FAT TUESDAY (@fattuesdayart) in 2019 (Figures 5 and 6).

How to Steal a Culture was performed and exhibited at Columbia College Chicago's Black Arts Festival in 2018 (Figure 1).

For Your Pleasure was exhibited December 2017 to January 2018 at C33 Gallery for Columbia College Chicago (Figures 4 and 7).

"A Liberated Black Beauty" was published in *READY Publication* (2017).

"Me, My Fat, and I" was published for Porkbelly Press's *Love Me, Love My Belly* zine no. 3 (2017).

"What Will Follow" was published in Ohioana Library Association's *Ohioana Quarterly* vol. 58, no. 4 (2015).

Additionally, I would like to acknowledge Megan Kirby for providing the first, second, and third images in the "Flesh" section of this book.

21st CENTURY ESSAYS
David Lazar and Patrick Madden, Series Editors

This series from Mad Creek Books is a vehicle to discover, publish, and promote some of the most daring, ingenious, and artistic nonfiction. This is the first and only major series that announces its focus on the essay—a genre whose plasticity, timelessness, popularity, and centrality to nonfiction writing make it especially important in the field of nonfiction literature. In addition to publishing the most interesting and innovative books of essays by American writers, the series publishes extraordinary international essayists and reprint works by neglected or forgotten essayists, voices that deserve to be heard, revived, and reprised. The series is a major addition to the possibilities of contemporary literary nonfiction, focusing on that central, frequently chimerical, and invariably supple form: The Essay.

---

*Annual Gournay Prize Winner